THE SOCIETY FOR THE STUDY OF EGYPTIAN ANTIQUITIES (SSEA)

STUDIES

NO. 5

The Pottery of Daily Life in Ancient Egypt

Patricia Paice

BENBEN PUBLICATIONS
MISSISSAUGA

Published by
Benben Publications / SSEA Publications
1483 Carmen Drive
Mississauga, Ontario
CANADA   L5G 3Z2

Printed in Canada

ISBN 0-920808-02-6
ISSN 0825-4699

THE POTTERY OF DAILY LIFE IN ANCIENT EGYPT [1]

Traditional history, with its concern for the short time span, for the individual and the event, has long accustomed us to the headlong, dramatic, breathless rush of its narrative.

The new economic and social history puts cyclical movement in the forefront of its research and is committed to that time span....So today, side by side with traditional narrative history, there is an account of conjunctures which lays open large sections of the past, ten, twenty, fifty years at a stretch ready for examination.

Far beyond this second account we find a history capable of traversing even greater distances, a history to be measured in centuries this time: the history of the long, even of the very long time span, of the *longue durée*.[2]

Introduction

The pottery vessels excavated by archaeologists can tell us nothing about "event history" or individual time, but they are not so changeless that they should be considered part of the "*longue durée*" or geographical time. Rather, pottery vessels are material evidence for economic and social history - "a history of gentle rhythms, of groups and groupings", "deep-running currents", "economies and states, societies and civilizations".[3]

Until relatively recently the utilitarian domestic pottery of Egypt has been neglected in publications. The more beautiful and unique whole vessels were chosen for illustration leaving the everyday domestic wares largely unrepresented and, since most published pottery came from tombs, it followed that little was known about the pottery used in regular subsistence activities. Recent publications have added to the corpus of domestic pottery available for study, but not for every period nor for every type of context. Therefore the scenes of daily life in tomb paintings provide a valuable additional source of information. These pictures portray daily activities, including the preparation and serving of food, so that the tomb owner could continue to enjoy the benefits of such activities after death. Therefore the scenes should portray real life as the tomb artist saw it.

The tomb scenes will be studied with the aim of answering these questions:

1. *Can function be assigned to specific pottery forms on the basis of their appearance in scenes of daily life?*

2. *Can a study of the types of activity scenes which use pottery vessels help to identify activity areas found in excavation?*

3. *Do the examples of vessels portrayed in Egyptian tomb representations resemble actual excavated pottery of the same period?*

Parameters for the Study

It seems reasonable to expect that vessels depicted in scenes where people are engaged in normal daily and seasonal activities have been portrayed realistically (even if sketchily). In this case these daily life scenes might be regarded as a source of ethnographic data supplied by a contemporary observer - the tomb artist. The two parameters used in selecting tomb scenes for analysis were that the scenes depict everyday activities involving the use of pottery vessels, and that the function of the vessels be clearly indicated by the context. Only then is it possible to associate particular functions with specific vessel forms. All formal, religious, ritual, offering, and libation tomb scenes were eliminated from the study on the grounds that the vessels were often made of stone or metal, and that such vessels could be portrayed in a stylized manner.

Procedure

An extensive review of published Egyptian tombs was undertaken to locate those with depictions of daily life.[4]   A second level of selection eliminated those scenes which did not feature pottery in the activities portrayed. At the end of the process, I was left with 18 Old Kingdom, 10 Middle Kingdom, and 27 New Kingdom tombs which fulfilled the criteria for the study. Each of these 55 tombs was decorated with one or more scenes in which pottery was used in routine daily and seasonal activities. (See Catalogue Appendix A.)

The scenes from the tombs in this catalogue were then grouped by both time period and activity. A chronological list of all relevant tombs was prepared indicating the types of activity in which pottery use was depicted (Old Kingdom: Figure 1; Middle Kingdom: Figure 2; New Kingdom: Figure 3.). The scenes fell into several clearly defined categories most of which can be related to the production, preparation, and consumption of food, and to workshop activities. The following discussion centres on those scenes which depict food-related activities.[5]

Each one of the scenes shown in Figures 4 to 10 below is representative of others of the same type and the discussion is representative of the group, not only the individual examples shown in the illustrations. Examination of these groups enabled the researcher to identify those activities which depended on the use of pottery vessels and, within these specified activities, to identify the characteristic forms of pottery used for a particular function.

Food Production

Milking (Figure 4)[6]

Two types of pottery vessels are illustrated in connection with the milking process, a large bowl for collection of the milk and a milk jar for transportation.

Old Kingdom milking scenes show the cow milked into a rounded bowl similar to a cooking bowl (see Figure 9). This bowl could not be carried far, but is sometimes shown in use to feed a nearby calf. For transportation away from the milking site the milk is transferred to a special kind of jar depicted with a neck and flaring rim to which a rope handle was attached. Some of the milk jars in these scenes are depicted with a flat base and could stand unsupported, others are shown with a rounded base and could not stand alone. Middle Kingdom scenes show similar jars in use with constricted necks but without the flaring rim.

Milking scenes are lacking in the catalogue of New Kingdom tombs; however, milk jars are frequently shown being carried by cattle herders. Most New Kingdom milk jars are depicted with flat bases. The basic shape of these milk jars had changed little from the earlier periods. The design with a constricted neck to which a rope handle is attached was well suited to the function that this vessel was required to perform, in that the milk would not easily spill while carried by the herder.

Watering and Water Carrying (Figure 5)[7]

Food production depends on a supply of water for the crops. Watering jars are the only pottery vessels depicted in watering scenes.

Tomb scenes show garden plots being watered from two globular jars suspended from a yoke on a man's shoulders. This method of watering is shown in tombs from the Old, Middle,

FIGURE 1   Chronological List of Tombs: Old Kingdom

OLD KINGDOM		BREAD MAKING	BREWING	VINTAGE	COOKING	DRINKING	WATERING GARDEN	CARRYING WATER	MILKING	FEEDING ANIMALS	POTTERS WORKSHOP	MARKET	SCRIBES
Reign	*Tomb owner*												
Dynasty IV													
Mycerinus	*Mersyankh*	X	X			X							
Dynasty V													
Ne-User-Re	*Urarna*				X						X		
	Nianchnum+Chnumhotep	X	X	X	X		X		X			X	
	Nefer + Ka-Hay			X									
Djed-ka-Re	*Ptahhetep*			X									
	Akhethetep			X					X				
	Ti	X	X					X	X				
Dynasty VI													
Teti	*Shedu*				X								
	Asa	X	X							X			
Teti / Pepi I	*Khentika*	X	X										
Pepy II	*Idu*	X	X		X								
	Khenty	X	X										
	Mera	X	X					X					
	Pepi		X		X								
	Pepiankh the Middle	X	X										
	Pepiankh			X	X								
	Aba				X				X				X
	Zau												X

FIGURE 2   Chronological List of Tombs: Middle Kingdom

MIDDLE KINGDOM		BREAD MAKING	BREWING	VINTAGE	COOKING	REFRESHMENT OUTDOORS	WATERING GARDEN	CARRYING WATER	MILKING	FEEDING ANIMALS	POTTERS WORKSHOP	WEAVING	LEATHER WORK
Reign	Tomb owner												
Dynasty XI													
	Kemsit								X				
	Baqt II				X								
	Baqt III	X		X							X	X	
	Khety			X								X	
Dynasty XI-XII	Daga	X	X										
Dynasty XII													
Amenemhet I	Senbi								X				
Senwosret I	Amenemhat	X	X	X	X		X				X		X
	Antefoker	X	X		X	X	X	X					
Senwosret II	Khnumhotep	X	X				X			X	X	X	
Senwosret II/ Senwosret III	Tehutihetep	X	X				X	X			X	X	

FIGURE 3   Chronological List of Tombs: New Kingdom

NEW KINGDOM		BREAD MAKING	BREWING	VINTAGE	WINE TRANSPORT	WINE STORAGE	BANQUET	REFRESHMENT OUTDOORS	WATERING GARDEN	CARRYING WATER	MILK	HONEY	PRESERVING FOWL	MARKET	BRICK MAKING	INCENSE PRODUCTION	BRAZIER
Reign	*Tomb owner*																
Dynasty XVIII																	
Tuth.II/Hat/Tuth.III	*Paheri*			X			X						X				
Hatshepsut/Tuth.III	*Antef*			X	X	X											
Hat/Tuth.III/Am.II	*Benja*				X						X	X					
Tuthmosis III	*Amenmose (42)*						X										
	Amenemhet						X										
Tuthmosis III/Am.II	*Menkheperesonb*				X	X											
	Amenmose (89)															X	
	Rekhmire	X	X	X	X	X	X		X			X	X		X		
Tuth.III/Am.II/T.IV	*Tjanuni*						X	X		X							
Amenophis II	*Nebamun (17)*	X	X				X										
	Kenamun	X	X			X											
Amenophis II/T.IV	*Nakht*			X			X	X					X				
Tuthmosid	*Dhout*						X										
Tuthmosis IV	*Djeserkeresonb*				X			X		X							
	Amenhotep						X										
	Nebamun (90)			X		X	X										
Akhenaten	*Ahmes*						X										
	Ay	X					X										
	Huya						X	X									
	Mahu						X										X
	Meryra						X	X									
	Parennefer			X	X	X	X										
	Ramose				X						X	X					
Tutankhamun	*Khons*										X	X					
Ay	*Neferhotep*			X	X	X	X	X			X	X		X			
Dynasty XIX																	
Rameses II	*Apy*			X		X	X										
	Nakhtamun						X										

FIGURE 4   Milking Scenes

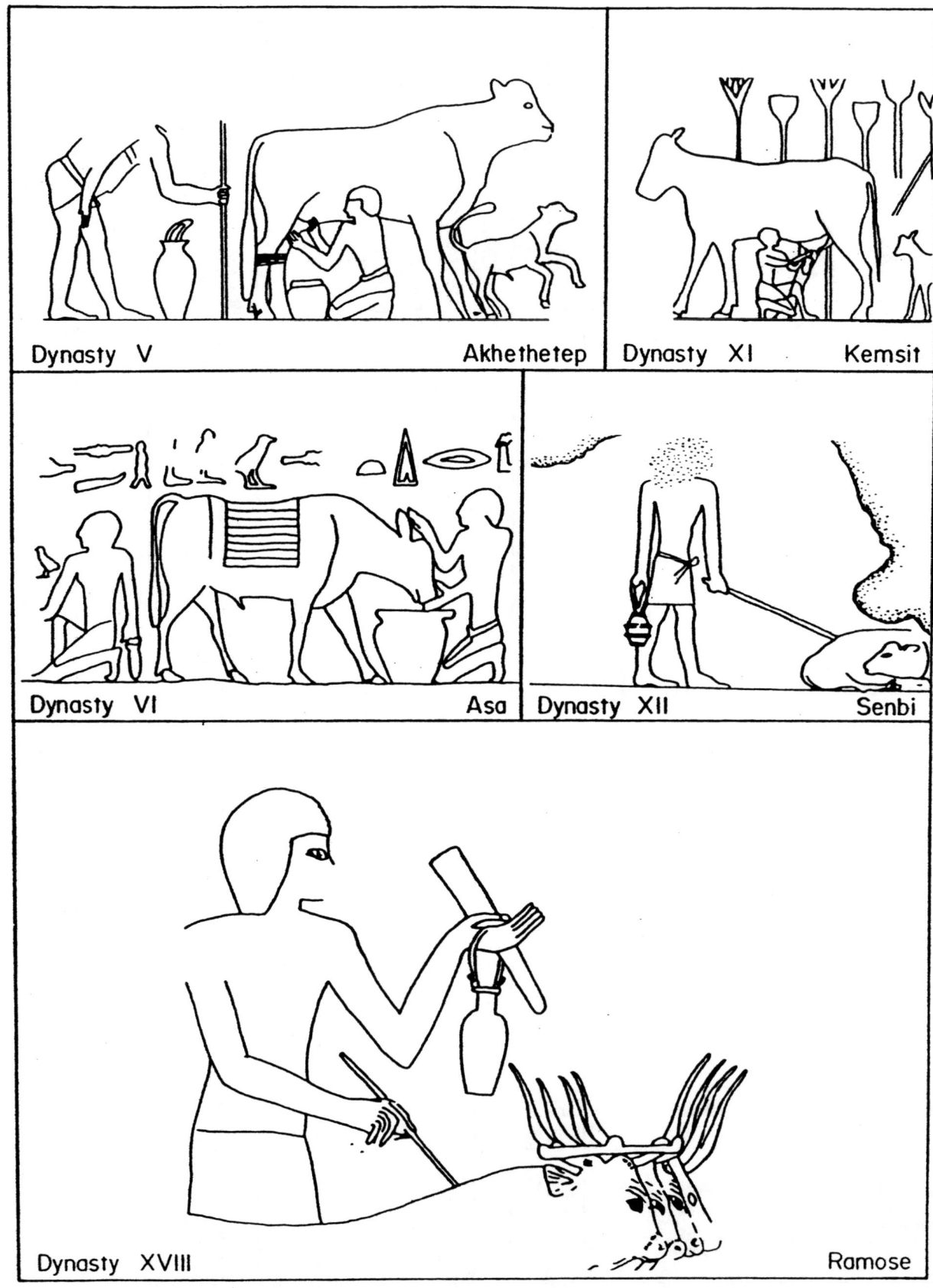

Dynasty V   Akhethetep

Dynasty XI   Kemsit

Dynasty VI   Asa

Dynasty XII   Senbi

Dynasty XVIII   Ramose

FIGURE 5 Watering and Water Carrying Scenes

Dynasty V — Nianchchnum † Chnumhotep

Dynasty XII — Khnumhotep

Dynasty XII — Tehutihetep

Dynasty XVIII — Ramose

and New Kingdoms. Other shapes of jar could be used as long as they had a constricted neck to prevent accidental spillage and for the attachment of a rope. The same arrangement is also illustrated in New Kingdom scenes where small containers of water are being transported. However, in this case, the jars would not need to be tipped over to release their water, so they could be supported more securely in rope netting slung from the carrying poles.

Food Processing

Bread-Making (Figure 6)[8]

The activities of bread-making and brewing are always portrayed side by side, probably because the initial stages, which required no pottery containers were common to both.[9] However, when the two processes of bread-making and beer-making diverged, pottery containers became an essential part of the manufacturing process. In the first stage of the process a worker is depicted crushing the grain in a mortar using a long pestle from a standing position. In the second stage the crushed grain is placed on a grinding stone set in the floor and a kneeling worker is shown using a stone roller to grind it to flour. Then the flour can be collected and made into a dough. At this point the dough could be either placed in pottery moulds for baking or it could be shaped by hand into loaves of different shapes and baked as bread.

Two types of vessel are illustrated in bread making scenes, a bulk container for dough and the small bread moulds for baking. In the Old Kingdom scenes, the bread moulds are pre-heated in a stack over the fire, then the dough is put into the hot moulds and allowed to bake as the moulds cooled. The bread moulds of the IVth and Vth Dynasties are shown with an inverted bell shape, giving the appearance of having being formed in the palm of the hand. By the early VIth Dynasty the pottery moulds are portrayed with a flat base, but are otherwise unchanged. In the late VIth Dynasty, the flat base is sometimes shown lengthened into a knob-like projection.[10] The bulk container for dough is an open bowl in the IVth and Vth Dynasty scenes but is shown as a barrel-shaped vessel in scenes of the VIth Dynasty.[11]

Middle Kingdom bakery scenes show the bread mould as a straight-sided cone with a flat base. The bread moulds are still being heated in a stack over a fire.[12] The XIth Dynasty scenes show fairly substantial conical bread moulds, while the XIIth Dynasty moulds are thinner and more cylindrical. The Middle Kingdom scenes include a tall barrel-shaped vessel with a rolled rim as the bulk container for dough.

Bread moulds of a long cone shape continue to be illustrated in New Kingdom tomb scenes, preserving the general shape of the Middle Kingdom examples. But the New Kingdom bread moulds seem to be of larger diameter and are usually shown with a rounded base or equipped with a peg base. Large, round-bottomed jars with a neck and flaring rim are used as bulk containers in the bakery. They are often shown tipped to one side for ease of access.

Brewing (Figure 7)[13]

Workers in brewing scenes are shown forcing pieces of dough through a sieve into a water-filled vat. The resulting mash is allowed to ferment and then either decanted or strained into beer jars. Three types of vessels are required for this process, large fermentation jars, pouring vessels, and beer storage jars. The IVth Dynasty fermenting vessel is a large open vat or bowl similar to the bulk containers for dough in the bakery. Likewise, the Vth and VIth Dynasty fermenting vessel is depicted as a wide-mouthed, barrel-shaped jar similar to the bulk container for dough in contemporary baking scenes.

A simple ovoid pouring jar without handles or spout is frequently used to transfer the beer into storage jars in Old Kingdom brewing scenes.

FIGURE 6   Baking Scenes

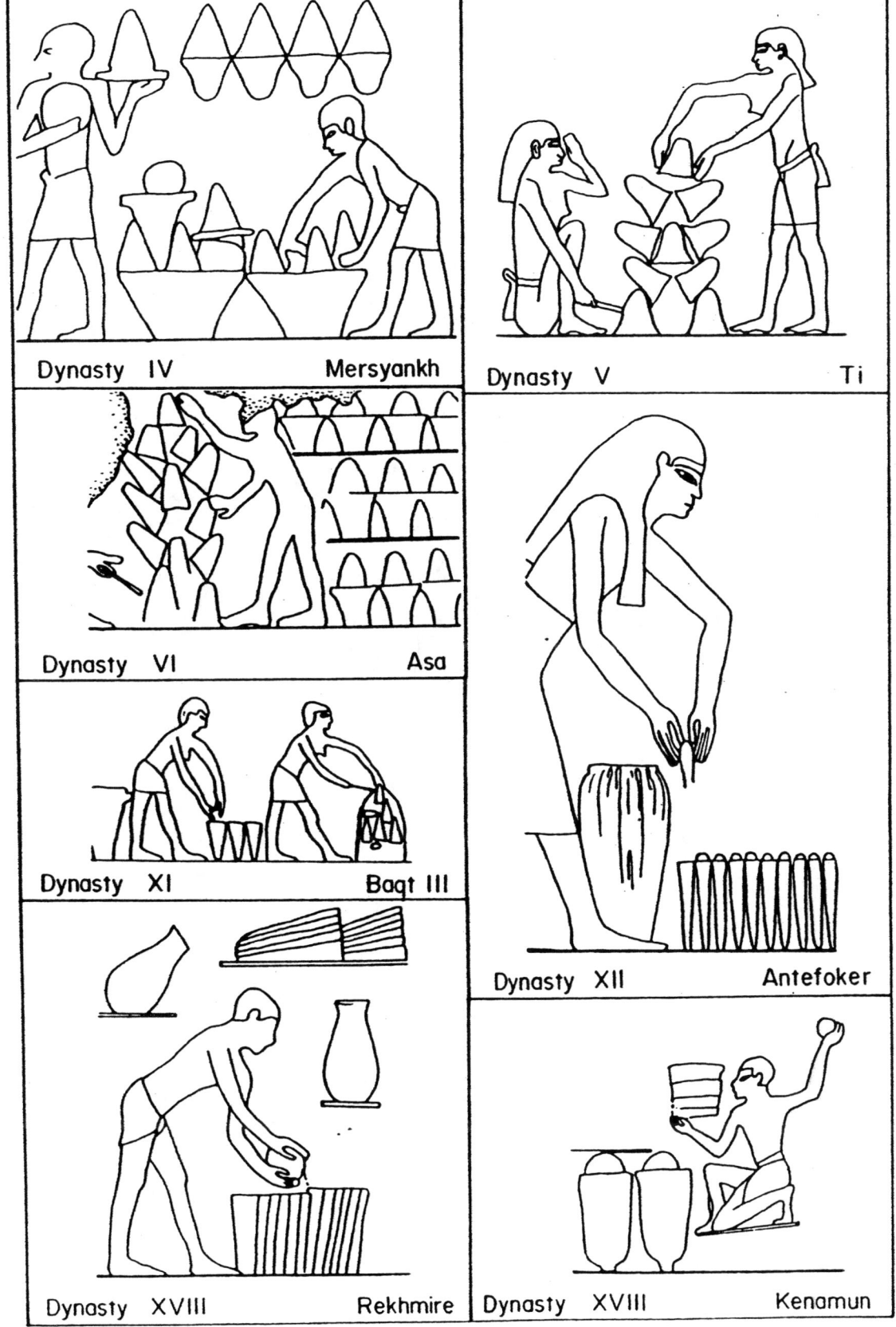

Dynasty IV   Mersyankh

Dynasty V   Ti

Dynasty VI   Asa

Dynasty XI   Baqt III

Dynasty XII   Antefoker

Dynasty XVIII   Rekhmire

Dynasty XVIII   Kenamun

FIGURE 7   **Brewing Scenes**

Dynasty IV   Mersyankh

Dynasty V   Akhethetep

Dynasty VI   Khenty

Dynasty VI   Khentika

Dynasty XII   Antefoker

Dynasty XVIII   Nebamun (17)

However, many pouring jars depicted in Old Kingdom tombs have a side spout, whatever the shape of the jar itself.[14]

In the IVth Dynasty scenes, the beer storage jars are shown as tall ovoid jars with a rolled rim and a flat base, similar to the wine jars of the period. The VIth Dynasty scenes show the beer jars with rounded or pointed bases and a more flaring rim.

The barrel-shaped fermenting vessel continues to be shown in scenes of the Middle Kingdom. However, the storage jars for beer in the Middle Kingdom scenes have changed markedly from their ovoid Old Kingdom predecessors. The new form is a large globular vessel with a small neck and a flaring rim which is sealed with a clay cap. The pouring jars have similarly changed from the small ovoid Old Kingdom vessels to small globular jars in Middle Kingdom brewing scenes.

The brewers featured in New Kingdom tomb scenes follow the traditional methods of forcing dough through a basket-work sieve into a large fermenting jar. This vessel has been altered from its previous barrel-shape by the addition of a neck, and in most cases the widest part of the jar has been shifted downward, creating a large round-bottomed vessel similar to the bulk containers for dough in New Kingdom baking scenes. This shape is a larger version of the contemporary beer storage jar.[15]
The round-bottomed beer storage jars of the New Kingdom brewing scenes are a graceful "carafe" shape which can be seen as a logical progression from the globular beer jars depicted in Middle Kingdom scenes, created by widening the mouth and lengthening the neck of the Middle Kingdom beer jars. (The presence in brewing scenes of smaller versions of the two-handled wine storage jar, described below, seems to indicate that these vessels could also be used for beer.) New Kingdom banquet scenes depict supplies of beer in simple round-bottomed "carafes" of a graceful shape positioned near the wine storage jars ready for the

feast.[16] The beer "carafes" and the wine storage jars are shown with painted decoration beginning in the reign of Tuthmosis III.[17] Sometimes the beer can be seen foaming over the rim of the "carafe" and servants are employed in fanning the jars to keep the beer cool.[18]

Wine-Making (Figure 8)[19]

Wine-making scenes feature a similar range of pottery vessels to that used in brewing scenes, large fermenting vessels, small pouring jars, and storage jars.

In Old Kingdom vintage scenes, the fruit is squeezed into a low, rounded, closed-mouth bowl with a flat base.[20] The juice formed as a result of the pressing of the fruit is poured into ovoid storage containers, then sealed. Sometimes these storage containers are depicted with ledge handles, a characteristic of Early Bronze Age Palestinian pottery borrowed by the Egyptians, presumably after an extended period of commerce.[21] There were also jugs, again of Syro-Palestinian derivation, available for the wine. These had a single handle from the flat rim to the shoulder, and a pouring spout. Wine placed in these jugs may have been intended for immediate use, rather than for storage. Depictions of pouring vessels are similar to those for beer. Simple ovoid pouring vessels are featured along with jars or bowls having a side spout.

The Middle Kingdom vintage scenes show the grapes being squeezed into a low, everted, sloping-sided bowl or vat set into the ground. Then the wine is poured into tall, barrel-shaped jars which functioned as fermentation vats. The wine storage jars of the XIth Dynasty are illustrated as conical in shape and topped off with a conical cap (a mud jar sealing), portrayed as being striped. The store jars of the XIIth Dynasty seem to be taller with the neck sealed by a higher striped conical cap.

By the time of the New Kingdom, in place of squeezing the fruit, the vintage scenes always

FIGURE 8   Wine-making Scenes

Dynasty IV   Mersyankh

Dynasty V   Nianchchnum + Chnumhotep

Dynasty XI   Khety

Dynasty XII   Amenemhat

Dynasty XVIII   Nakht

Dynasty XVIII   Rekhmire

Dynasty XVIII   Parennefer

Dynasty XIX   Apy

feature the grapes being trodden by a group of men on a treading floor. The juice running out of the treading floor area through escape channels is placed directly into wine jars. The direct transference of the juice into the jars in which the wine was to be stored seems inappropriate. A close acquaintance with home wine-making leads me to the conclusion that the jars could not have been sealed at this point without the risk of explosion due to fermentation gases forming under pressure in the sealed wine jars. The clay caps used to seal these wine jars are sometimes shown stamped with seals of ownership. It may be that some artistic license was being exercised in the composition of vintage scenes: perhaps a primary fermentation phase has been left out in the interests of a more condensed sequence which could take place in one location. Home wine-making also features several "racking" stages where the liquid is decanted off from the various sediments which sink to the bottom. However, this did not necessarily take place in ancient wine-making procedures. It must be remembered that strainers were an important part of the wine service known from excavation of many ancient Near Eastern tombs, including that of Tutankhamun.

In the early XVIIIth Dynasty tomb scenes, there are two versions of the wine jar, one without handles and the other with two handles. Up to the reign of Amenophis II handleless wine jars are shown carried in nets slung from carrying poles.[22] Egyptian store jars had not been manufactured with handles before the XVIIIth Dynasty and initially most of the handled jars were probably imported Canaanite store jars.[23] A wall-painting from Tomb No. 62 at Thebes shows Syrian merchants unloading imported Canaanite jars and other goods from a ship.[24] Undoubtedly the Syrian wine was the important trade item, the jar just happened to be the container provided for a desired commodity. But the utility of the Canaanite design must have influenced Egyptian potters so that the store jar with two handles ultimately became the preferred design for locally manufactured store jars. After the reign of

Tuthmosis IV, all jars are shown with two handles. Usually the scenes show the wine jars being carried on the shoulder by a bearer holding the jar by both handles to assist in balance.

The wine jars portrayed in XIXth Dynasty tombs seem to be much narrower with very pointed bases. The same jars used to store wine could also function in a variety of other storage capacities. They have been portrayed as containers for different kinds of oils,[25] honey,[26] incense,[27] water for brick-making,[28] and as store jars for preserved fowl.[29] In most, if not all, such cases it seems probable that we are seeing the re-use of older wine jars. After the wine was consumed, a perfectly servicable jar was made available for re-use in a variety of different ways. Often the jars would have been returned to the vineyards to be refilled with the juice of the next vintage, but if containers were urgently required for another purpose then the empty wine jars could easily have been pressed into service.

Cooking (Figure 9)[30]

The range of pottery equipment used in cooking includes an oven or stove as well as cooking pots and braziers.

Fifth Dynasty cooking scenes show that meat and fish were cooked in a rounded cooking pot. Sometimes the pot is seen supported on a circular stove with lugs to allow the escape of hot gases between the rim of the stove and the lower part of the cooking pot. The VIth Dynasty scenes depict a larger version of this cooking pot with a wider mouth, flaring out more from the base. It is supported on a stove or oven which has a "tripod" arm support for the vessel, again allowing for the escape of gases. In Old Kingdom scenes the fowl is roasted on a spit over a low, flaring, pan brazier filled with charcoal, while the cook wields a fan over the flames.

In the Middle Kingdom scenes, most

FIGURE 9 Cooking Scenes

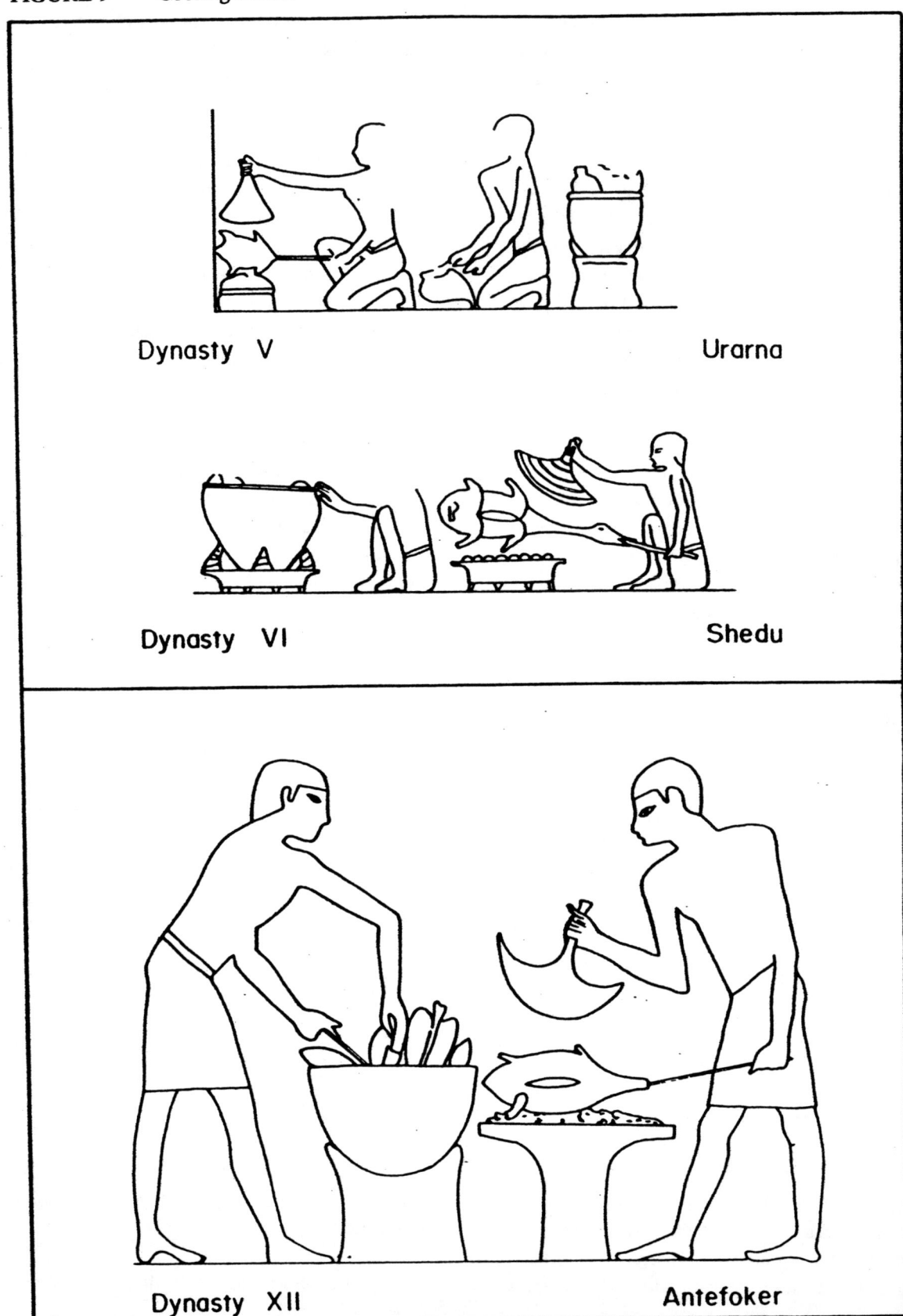

Dynasty V   Urarna

Dynasty VI   Shedu

Dynasty XII   Antefoker

cooking is done in a wide-mouthed, round-bottomed cooking pot with no discernable rim. A new design of stove elevates the cooking-pot so that the workers no longer have to squat while attending to their tasks. The charcoal-filled brazier for cooking fowl is similarly elevated so that the cook can stand. Scenes of cooking fish, meat, or fowl are rare in the New Kingdom corpus of tomb paintings, either through the random chance of preservation or due to changing fashions in tomb decoration.

Consumption of Food and Drink
(Figure 10)[31]

The pottery vessels depicted in scenes of eating and drinking include pouring vessels, ring stands, juglets and drinking bowls or cups.

The Dynasty IV scene shows a man drinking from a small ovoid jar similar to a pouring vessel from the brewing and wine-making scenes of the period. The Dynasty XII scene of drinking in the fields shows a similar jar but with a barely discernable neck. It could be called a cylindrical beaker with a round base. Eating and drinking were rarely depicted in Old Kingdom or Middle Kingdom tomb decoration.

In contrast, the New Kingdom tombs depict numerous banquet scenes. Wine jars, beer jars, and water jars are all available for the feast, often adorned with fresh green plants. The wine jars are decanted into pouring jars, which are illustrated as simple cylindrical vessels or situlae with no neck and no handles. These serving jars could be placed directly in front of the guest on a ring stand, and servants are shown in attendance to pour the liquid from the situlae into small drinking cups or bowls held in the hand of the guest. The maid-servants who serve the women often carry one or two small juglets, ready to pour the contents into the drinking cup. The capacity of these juglets seems too small to fill the cup, therefore the contents were probably an addition of flavour or scent to the wine already in the cup.[32]

Types of Activities that Habitually
Use Pottery

Although the types of activities portrayed using pottery containers are consistent through time, there are changing emphases on the types of scenes chosen to decorate a tomb. (Figure 11)

In the food production category, milking scenes were common in Old and Middle Kingdom tombs, but not in New Kingdom tombs. Milk jars were carried by New Kingdom cattle herders, but the milking itself was not depicted. Scenes which show the watering of garden plots were repeated in each period.

The commonest category of tomb paintings which used pottery as an essential part of the process are food preparation scenes. The Old and Middle Kingdom tombs placed heavy emphasis on scenes showing bread-making and brewing. The New Kingdom tombs tended to highlight the production, transport, and storage of wine. Cooking scenes were common in the Old and Middle Kingdom tombs, but not in the New Kingdom.

The consumption of food and drink would inevitably require the use of pottery containers - the usual range of dinnerware - cups, bowls, dishes and plates would be expected. Unfortunately the tomb paintings of the Old Kingdom and Middle Kingdom are not a good source of depictions of these containers in actual use, although some are shown in formal settings and placed on offering tables. New Kingdom representations are more numerous and provide a better corpus of forms for the vessels used in food consumption.

Obviously all these activities of food production, processing, preparation, and consumption were practised whether they were depicted in tomb paintings or not. The pottery containers associated with these activities were in continual production and use. However, the pictorial evidence for these activities fluctuates with

FIGURE 10   Scenes of Pouring and Drinking

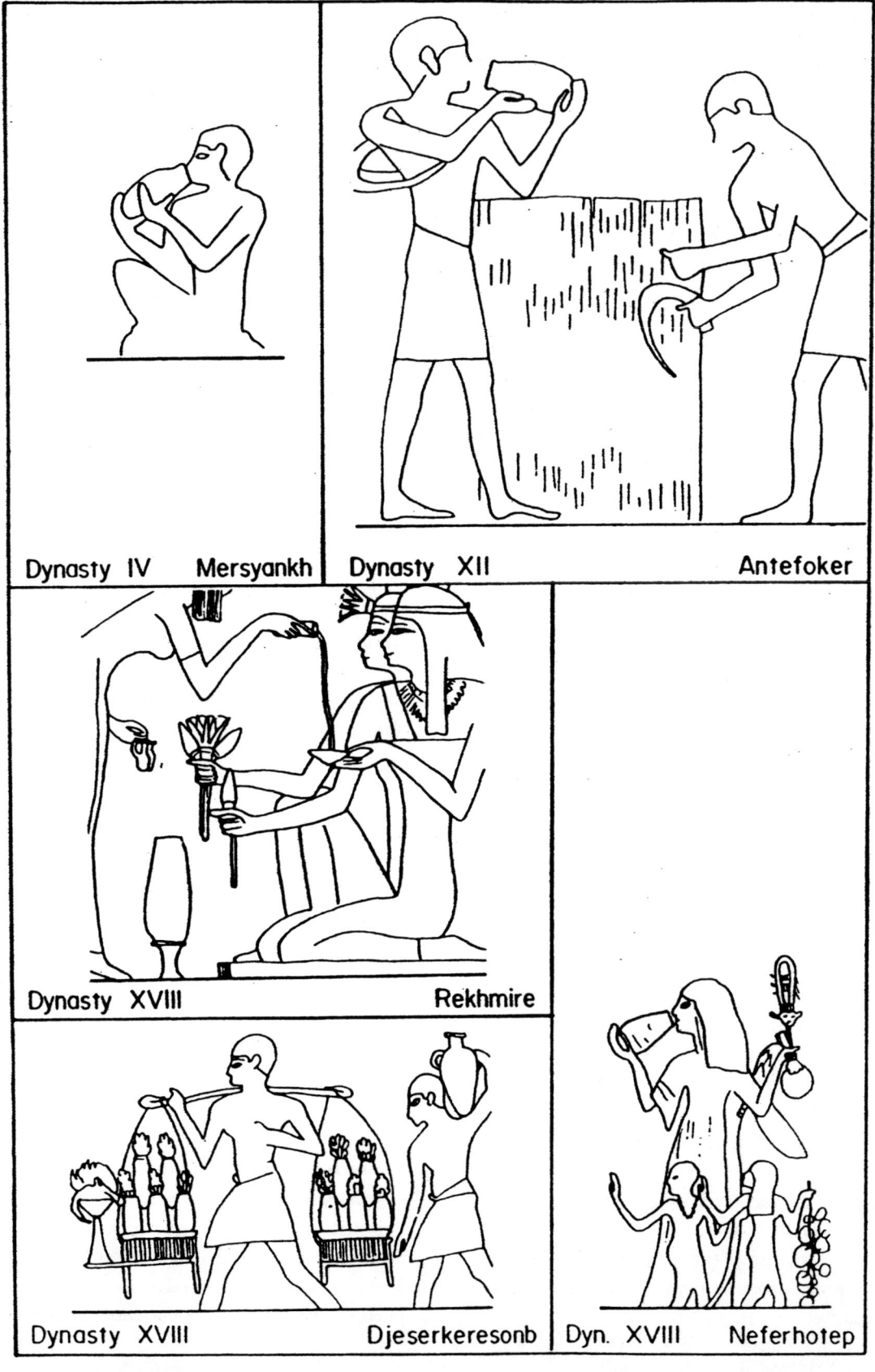

Dynasty IV   Mersyankh

Dynasty XII   Antefoker

Dynasty XVIII   Rekhmire

Dynasty XVIII   Djeserkeresonb

Dyn. XVIII   Neferhotep

FIGURE 11   Activities Portrayed in Tomb Scenes

Scene	Old Kingdom	Middle Kingdom	New Kingdom
	18 tombs	*10 tombs*	*27 tombs*
Milking Carrying milk jars	**** **	**	 ****
Watering garden Carrying water jars	* *	**** **	* *****
Bread making Brewing	******** *********	****** *****	**** ***

Wine making - Vintage
Wine jars -   stamping
               transport
               storage
	*****	***	********
			*
			********
			*************

Honey production Honey containers	 *		* **
Preserving fowl Feeding animals	 **	 *	***

Cooking -   fish
               fowl
               meat
	***
	****
	**
		
		**
		*	

Drinking Refreshment outdoors Banquet	*	 **	** *** ***************
Potters workshop Market Brick making Weaving Leather work Incense production Perfume production	* *	**** **** * *	 * * * *
Scribes water pot Brazier	**		 *

the prevalence of tomb paintings, and therefore is stronger at periods of prosperity evidenced by lavishly decorated tombs.

Analysis

We can now attempt to provide answers for the original questions.

1. *Can vessels be defined according to function?*

A catalogue of pottery shown in pictures of daily life has been compiled from a large number of Egyptian tombs over an extended period of time providing a reasonably significant data base. The material depicted by the Egyptian tomb artist can be used with success as an ethnographic source. It is certainly possible to use the pottery represented in scenes of daily life as evidence of function for a particular form. But it must be recognized that although the form may be specific to a particular function, that function can operate in more than one context. For example, the primary function of store jars may be to contain wine, but wine is a commodity which is used up in a short period of time, leaving behind a very useful container. The jar may be sent back to be refilled with more wine or it can be pressed into service for a variety of other purposes. The same form of jar can be used to store oils, incense, honey, water, or preserved fowl. Similarly the "drinking" forms like situlae are also used as pouring vessels in the brewing and vintage scenes of the Old, Middle, and New Kingdoms, when workers transfer liquids from one container to another. Field labourers drink from such vessels, but New Kingdom banqueters drink from small drinking bowls - the difference between pouring the "amber nectar" into a glass and drinking it straight from the bottle. The banqueters are more genteel, besides which they have servants to keep them "topped up".

A large barrel-shaped jar can hold water for baking,[33] brewing,[34] or softening leather.[35]

A specific shape of cooking bowl can also hold food in another context, as a feeding bowl for animals.[36] All the alternative possibilities should be borne in mind when assigning function to pottery without context.

2. *Can the catalogue of tomb paintings be used to designate activity areas found in excavation?*

It can be shown that certain forms of pottery are specific to a particular function and some forms are interdependent, always being shown together in a specific activity. It seems reasonable to suggest that archaeologists should be able to use this information when assigning function to a particular area of the site. Certainly, ovens, bread moulds and baking trays for the ancient equivalent to the modern "pita" bread characterized baking areas of the Saite, Persian, and Hellenistic periods at Tell el-Maskhuta in the Wadi Tumilat.[37] Similarly, preliminary studies show a linkage between "Tell el-Yehudiyeh" juglets, small ring stands and other drinking equipment in certain areas of the Second Intermediate Period settlement at Tell el-Maskhuta.[38] At a minimum, and working from sherd materials alone, it seems possible to construct assemblages of related pottery forms that would make it possible to identify bakeries, breweries, kitchens, and other activity areas in each of the periods dealt with in this paper.

3. *Can excavated pottery be dated by comparing the forms to those in tomb representations and vice versa?*

Five types of vessels were selected for a preliminary attempt to illustrate the comparison of pottery vessels in tomb paintings with those from excavations:

1. Wine/store jars
2. Milk jars
3. Bread moulds
4. Globular water jars
5. Pouring/drinking vessels

FIGURE 12a   Store Jars

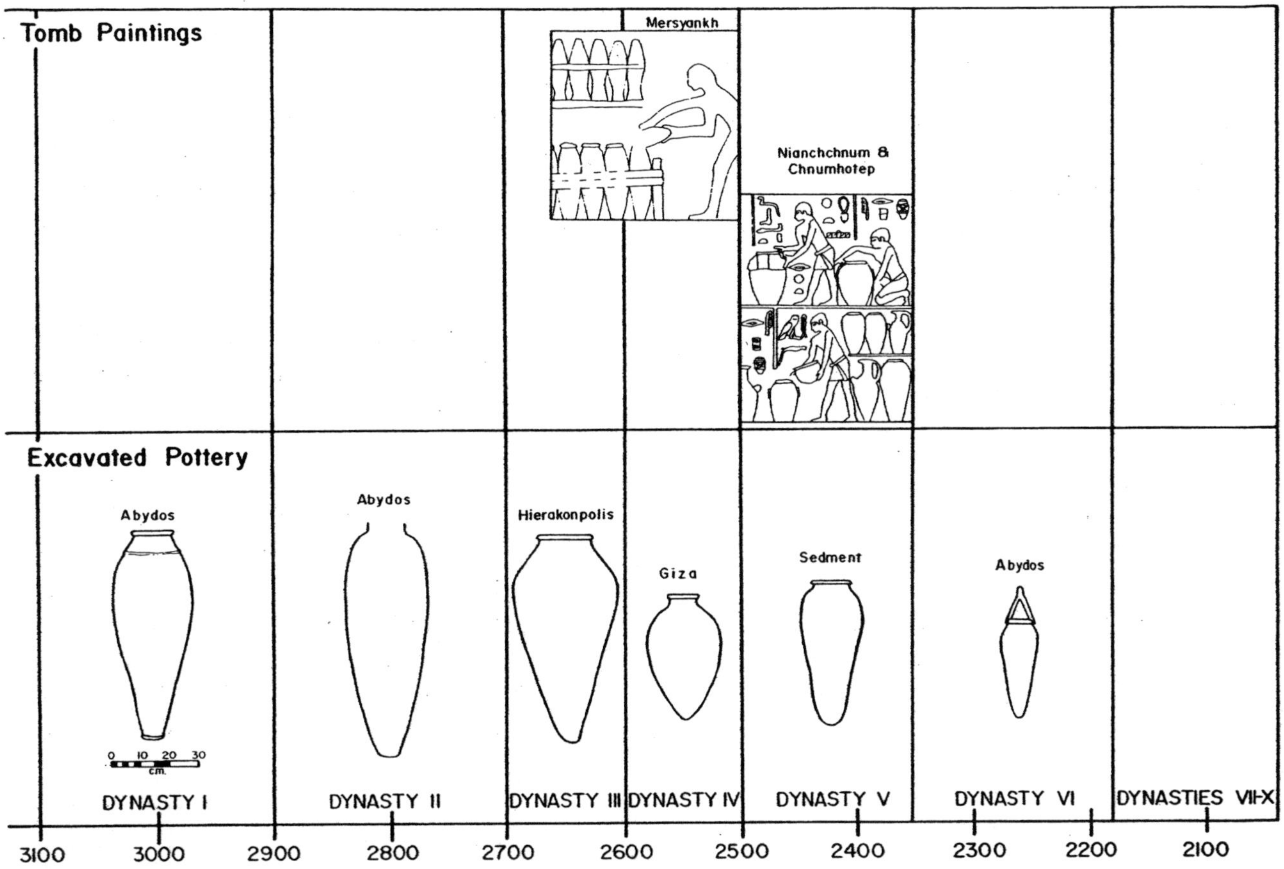

Tomb Paintings

Mersyankh

Nianchchnum &
Chnumhotep

Excavated Pottery

Abydos

Abydos

Hierakonpolis

Giza

Sedment

Abydos

0 10 20 30
cm

| DYNASTY I | DYNASTY II | DYNASTY III | DYNASTY IV | DYNASTY V | DYNASTY VI | DYNASTIES VII-X |

3100   3000   2900   2800   2700   2600   2500   2400   2300   2200   2100

FIGURE 13a   Milk Jars

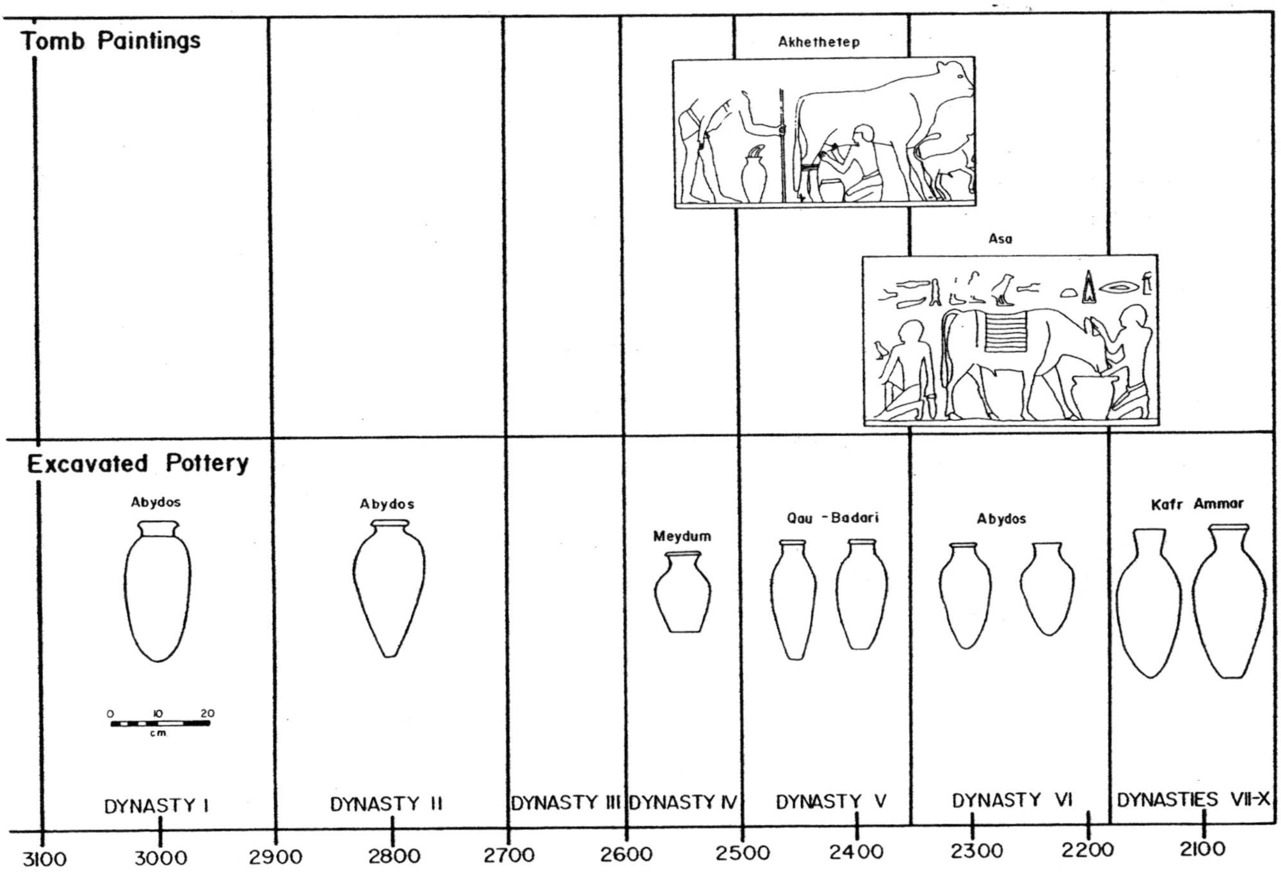

Tomb Paintings

Akhethetep

Asa

Excavated Pottery

Abydos

Abydos

Meydum

Qau - Badari

Abydos

Kafr Ammar

0   10   20
cm

| DYNASTY I | DYNASTY II | DYNASTY III | DYNASTY IV | DYNASTY V | DYNASTY VI | DYNASTIES VII-X |

3100   3000   2900   2800   2700   2600   2500   2400   2300   2200   2100

FIGURE 12b   Store Jars

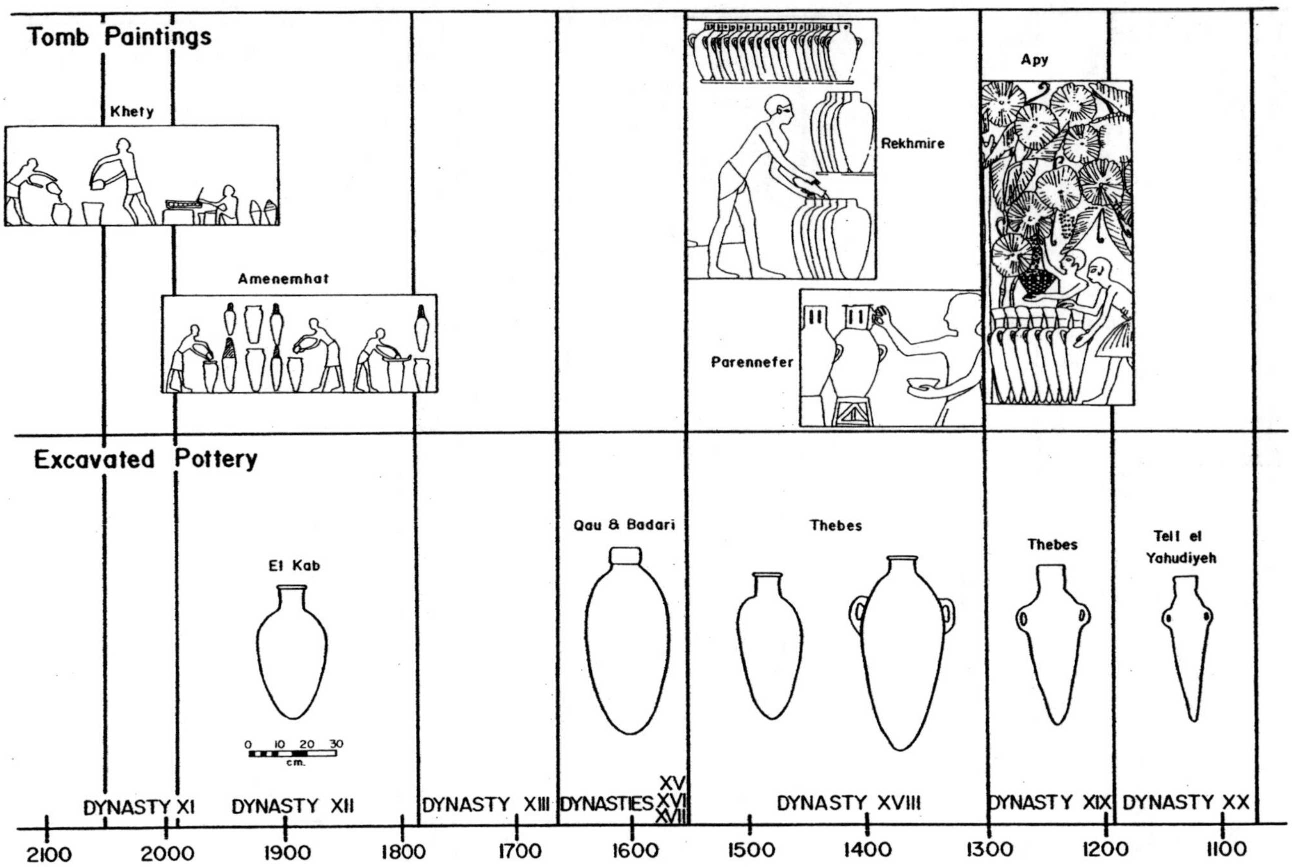

Tomb Paintings

Khety

Amenemhat

Rekhmire

Apy

Parennefer

Excavated Pottery

El Kab

0 10 20 30
cm.

Qau & Badari

Thebes

Thebes

Tell el Yahudiyeh

| DYNASTY XI | DYNASTY XII | DYNASTY XIII | DYNASTIES XV XVI XVII | DYNASTY XVIII | DYNASTY XIX | DYNASTY XX |

2100   2000   1900   1800   1700   1600   1500   1400   1300   1200   1100

FIGURE 13b   Milk Jars

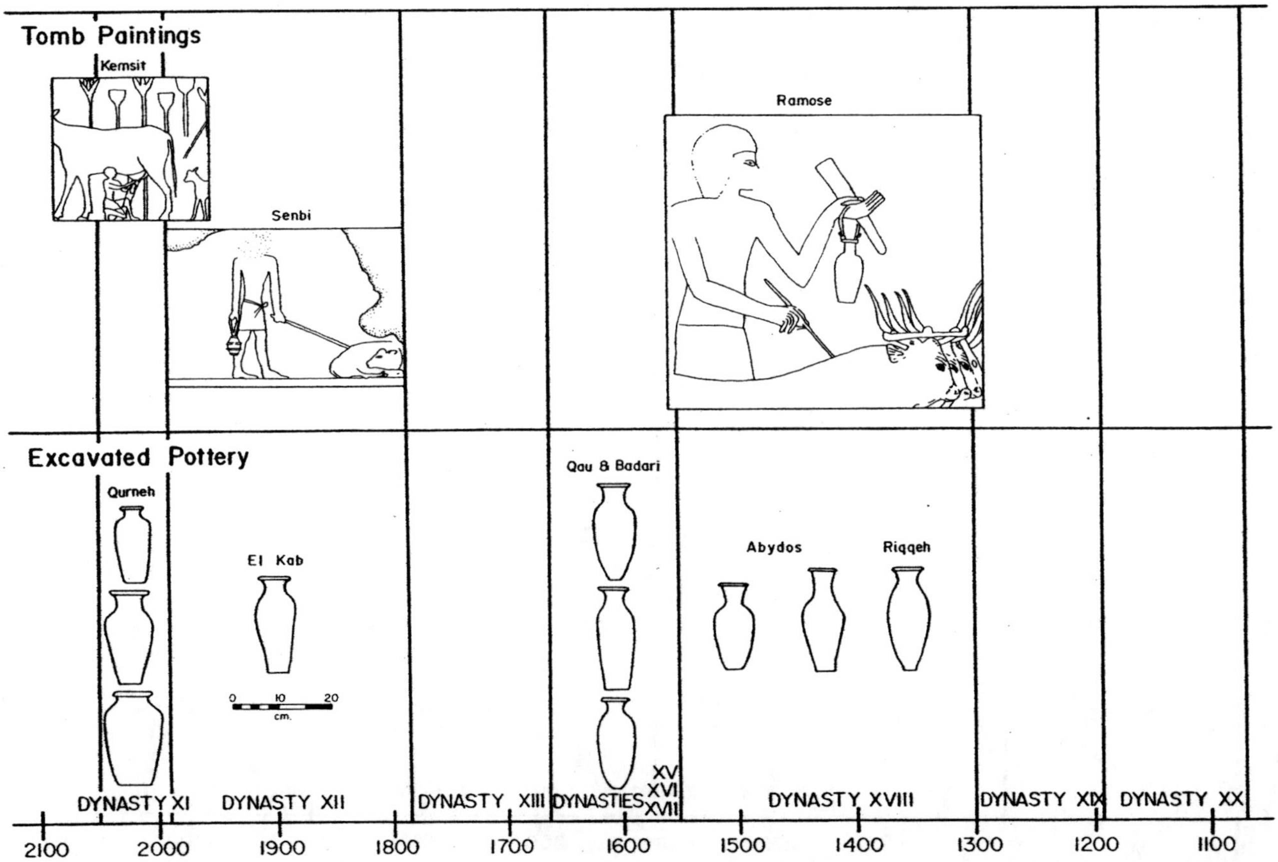

Tomb Paintings

Kernsit

Senbi

Ramose

Excavated Pottery

Qurneh

El Kab

0 10 20
cm.

Qau & Badari

Abydos

Riqqeh

| DYNASTY XI | DYNASTY XII | DYNASTY XIII | DYNASTIES XV XVI XVII | DYNASTY XVIII | DYNASTY XIX | DYNASTY XX |

2100   2000   1900   1800   1700   1600   1500   1400   1300   1200   1100

FIGURE 14a   Bread Moulds

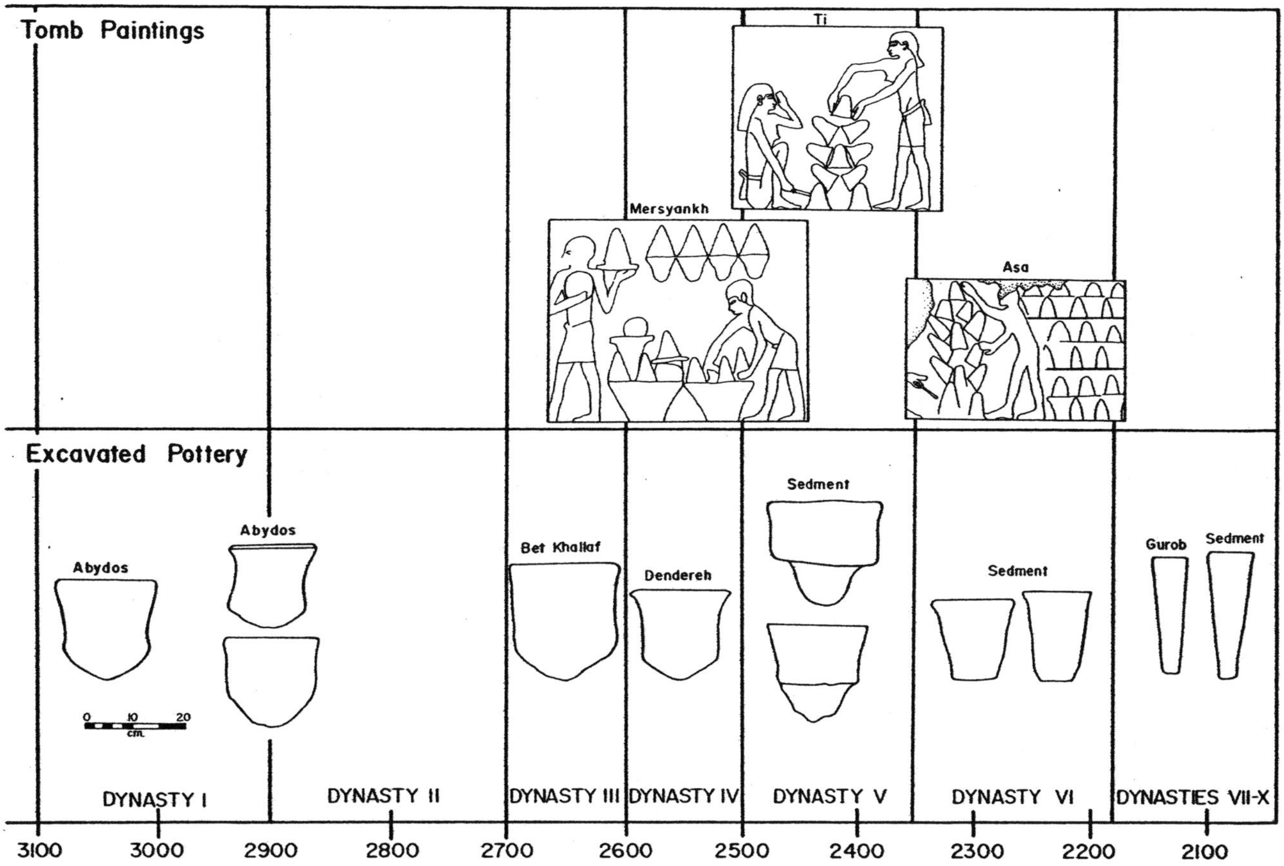

Tomb Paintings

Ti

Mersyankh

Asa

Excavated Pottery

Abydos

Abydos

Abydos

Bet Khallaf

Dendereh

Sedment

Sedment

Gurob   Sedment

0 10 20
cm.

| DYNASTY I | DYNASTY II | DYNASTY III | DYNASTY IV | DYNASTY V | DYNASTY VI | DYNASTIES VII-X |

3100   3000   2900   2800   2700   2600   2500   2400   2300   2200   2100

FIGURE 15a   Globular Jars

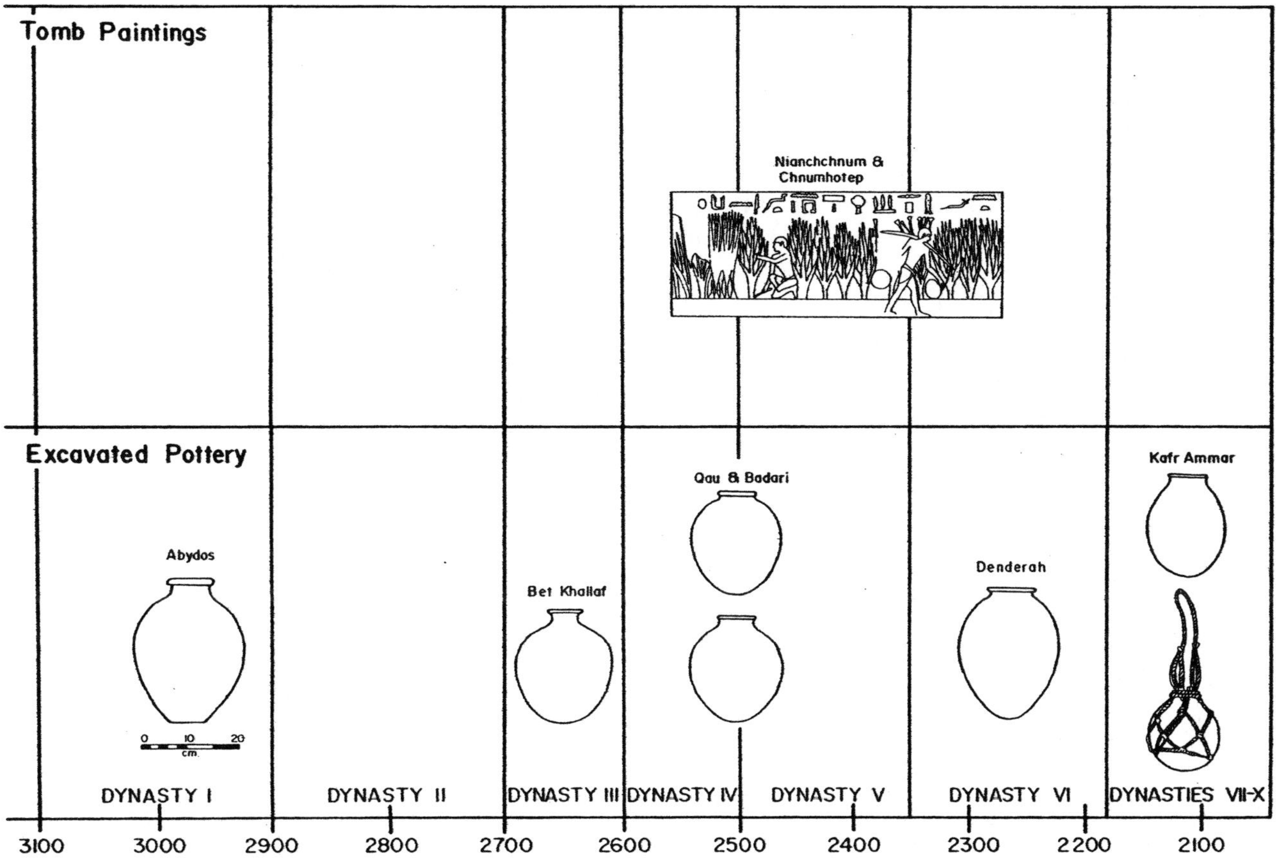

Tomb Paintings

Nianchchnum &
Chnumhotep

Excavated Pottery

Kafr Ammar

Abydos

Qau & Badari

Denderah

Bet Khallaf

0 10 20
cm.

| DYNASTY I | DYNASTY II | DYNASTY III | DYNASTY IV | DYNASTY V | DYNASTY VI | DYNASTIES VII-X |

3100   3000   2900   2800   2700   2600   2500   2400   2300   2200   2100

FIGURE 14b   Bread Moulds

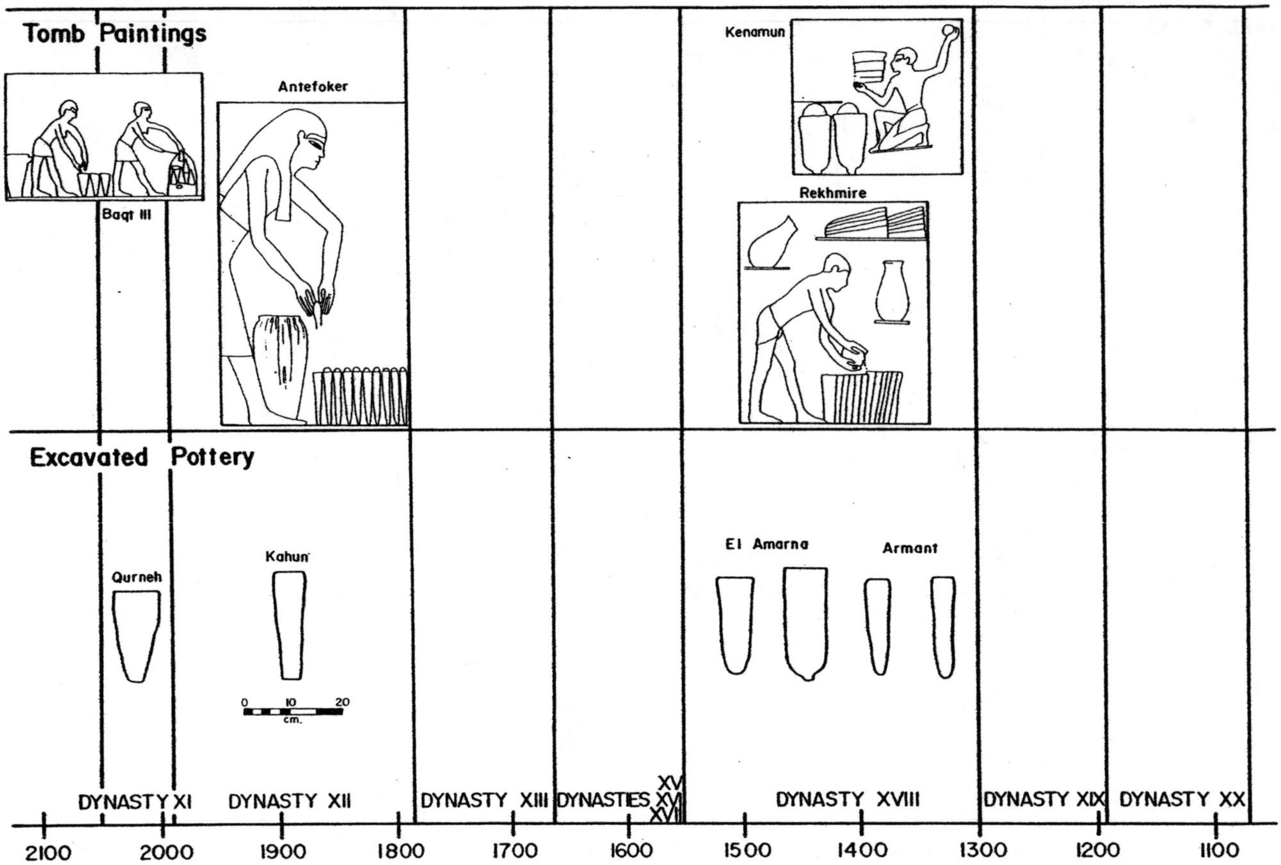

Tomb Paintings

Baqt III

Antefoker

Kenamun

Rekhmire

Excavated Pottery

Qurneh

Kahun

0   10   20
cm.

El Amarna   Armant

DYNASTY XI   DYNASTY XII   DYNASTY XIII   DYNASTIES XV XVI XVII   DYNASTY XVIII   DYNASTY XIX   DYNASTY XX

2100   2000   1900   1800   1700   1600   1500   1400   1300   1200   1100

FIGURE 15b   Globular Jars

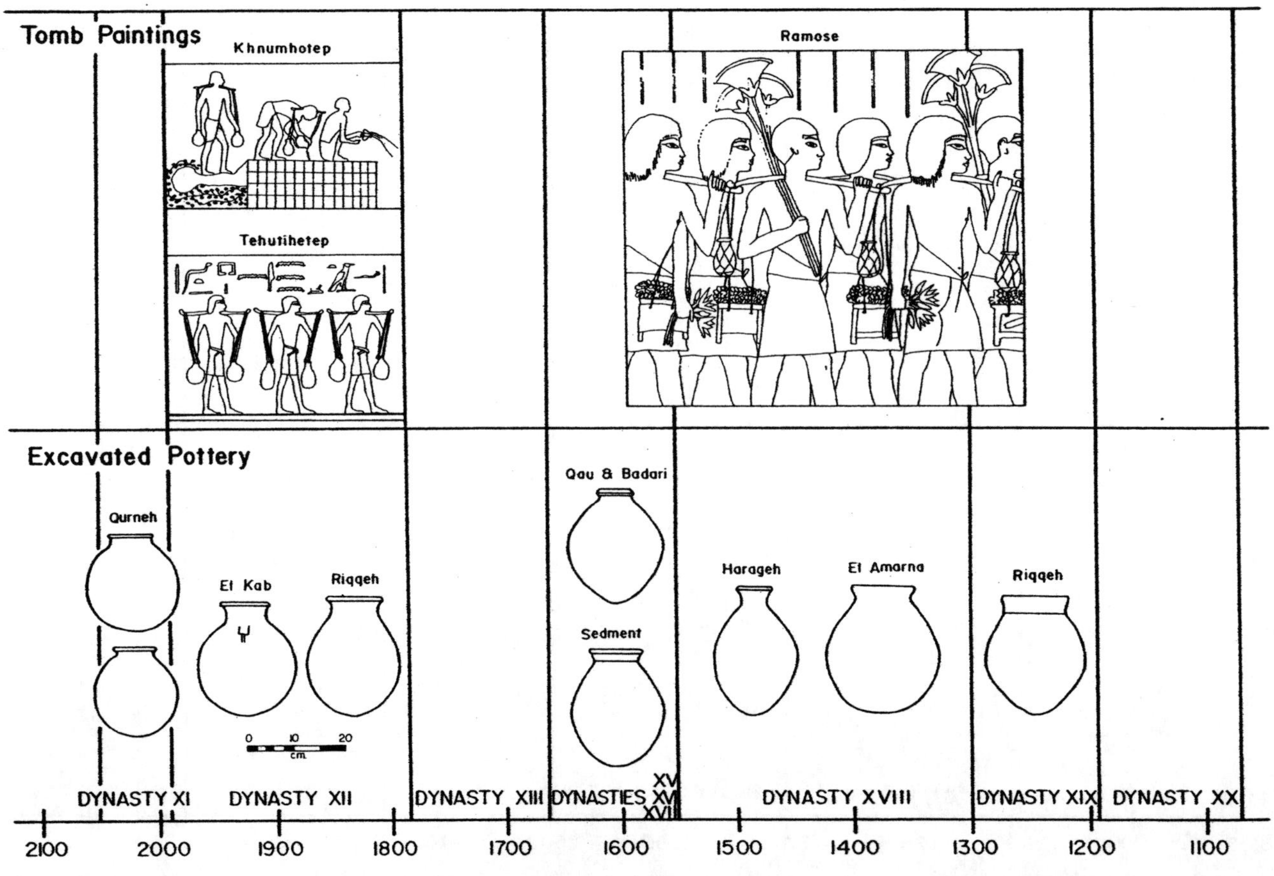

Tomb Paintings

Khnumhotep

Tehutihetep

Ramose

Excavated Pottery

Qurneh

El Kab   Riqqeh

0   10   20
cm.

Qau & Badari

Sedment

Harageh   El Amarna   Riqqeh

DYNASTY XI   DYNASTY XII   DYNASTY XIII   DYNASTIES XV XVI XVII   DYNASTY XVIII   DYNASTY XIX   DYNASTY XX

2100   2000   1900   1800   1700   1600   1500   1400   1300   1200   1100

The comparisons are displayed on a pair of chronological charts for each pottery type (Figures 12-16). Each chart shows a horizontal time line and is divided into two registers. The top register features tomb scenes for a period, while the bottom register displays examples of excavated pottery from the same period. The long chronological spread from 3100-1100 B.C. could not be incorporated on one page to show one uninterrupted line. The most convenient dividing point was the division between Old Kingdom and Middle Kingdom, ca.2100 B.C. Therefore, for each figure, a) is the Old Kingdom 3100-2100 B.C. and b) is the Middle Kingdom, Second Intermediate Period, and New Kingdom: 2100-1100 B.C. The pairs of charts show the development of five different types of vessels through two thousand years in a combination of tomb art and excavated pottery.[39]

In these charts, excavated pottery forms are present from the beginning of the time line, but tomb illustrations do not begin until after the first three dynasties. Lavishly decorated tombs are a feature of prosperous, settled times, therefore the First, Second, and Third Intermediate Periods are not well represented by tombs containing scenes of daily life. This is unfortunate, since the excavated pottery of those periods has not been closely dated. We will deal with each type of vessel in turn.

Store Jars (Figure 12a, 12b)

The basic store jar shape of the Old Kingdom is tall and ovoid with a rolled rim and rounded shoulders. The jars with a stumpy base excavated from Abydos and Hierakonpolis in Dynasty I-III contexts are reflected in the Dynasty IV tomb illustrations of Mersyankh. The jars with a rounded conical base predominated for the remainder of the Old Kingdom, from the IVth Dynasty store jars at Giza to the smaller VIth Dynasty store jars from Abydos.

It was not until Dynasty XII that a neck was added to the basic ovoid shape. This feature is present in the tomb illustrations of Khety and Amenemhat and the excavated store jars from El Kab. Handles were introduced on store jars during Dynasty XVIII, probably in response to the example set by the imported Canaanite store jars. The size of the store jar and thus its capacity had been reduced at the end of the Old Kingdom and again at the end of the New Kingdom. This reduction in the size of storage containers has already been noted in reviewing the tomb illustrations and may be a reflection of the economic climate of the times.

Milk Jars (Figure 13a, 13b)

Milk jars were small ovoid jars, characterised by a constricted neck, 3-6cm. in diameter, which is too small to insert a hand. Both flat and rounded bases can be demonstrated in the excavated pottery as well as in the tomb paintings. In the Old Kingdom, the base was flat in Akhethetep's tomb depiction and in the excavated jars from Meydum and Qau and Badari. The rounded base is shown in the tomb scene of Asa and in the excavated jars from Abydos.

In the Middle Kingdom the milk jar base was rounded in Kemsit's tomb, but flat in the drawings from the tomb of Senbi. The excavated jars from Qurneh and El-Kab had flat bases.

The XVIIIth Dynasty tomb of Ramose portrays a milk jar with a flat base like the excavated jars from Abydos and Riqqeh of the same period. With the examples from the tomb paintings before us, we can attempt to identify milk jars from the corpus of excavated pottery. For all periods it is possible to pick out a similar shape of jar with constricted neck in the size range depicted in the tomb paintings, ca. 20-30 cm. in length.

Bread Moulds (Figure 14a, 14b)

It will be remembered that the early bread moulds illustrated in Old Kingdom tombs were bell-shaped and gave the appearance of being formed in the palm of the hand. This shape is confirmed in the excavated pottery of Dynasties I-V from Abydos, Bet Khallaf, Dendereh, and Sedment.[40] The shape does not change much for the first five dynasties, or 700 years. It is not until Dynasty VI that the bread mould has a flat base, possibly as a result of being cut off a lump of clay. Again, this is confirmed by the Dynasty VI excavated vessels from Sedment. By the end of the First Intermediate Period the form has become an elongated cone seen in the excavated examples from Gurob and Sedment and the Middle Kingdom examples from Qurneh and Kahun. The next change perceived in the excavated pottery is the introduction of a rounded base in Dynasty XVIII bread moulds from El Amarna and Armant like those shown on their side in the tomb painting of Rekhmire. The El Amarna bread mould with a peg base could be a model for the one observable in a tomb painting of Kenamun.

Globular Jars (Figure 15a, 15b)

The favoured vessels for watering garden plots are a pair of globular jars suspended from a yoke. The rope attachment goes around the neck of the jar which has a thickened rim to hold the rope in position without slipping. For added security the attachment can be made to a rope net around the jar as in the excavated example from Kafr Ammar of the Xth Dynasty, and in a tomb painting of Ramose from the XVIIIth Dynasty.

We find that there are globular jars excavated from all periods, with the possible exception of Dynasties I and II, where there are no jars with rounded bases. The Early Dynastic jars with their flat bases cannot be called globular jars, but may have served a similar function.

FIGURE 16a   Pouring Vessels

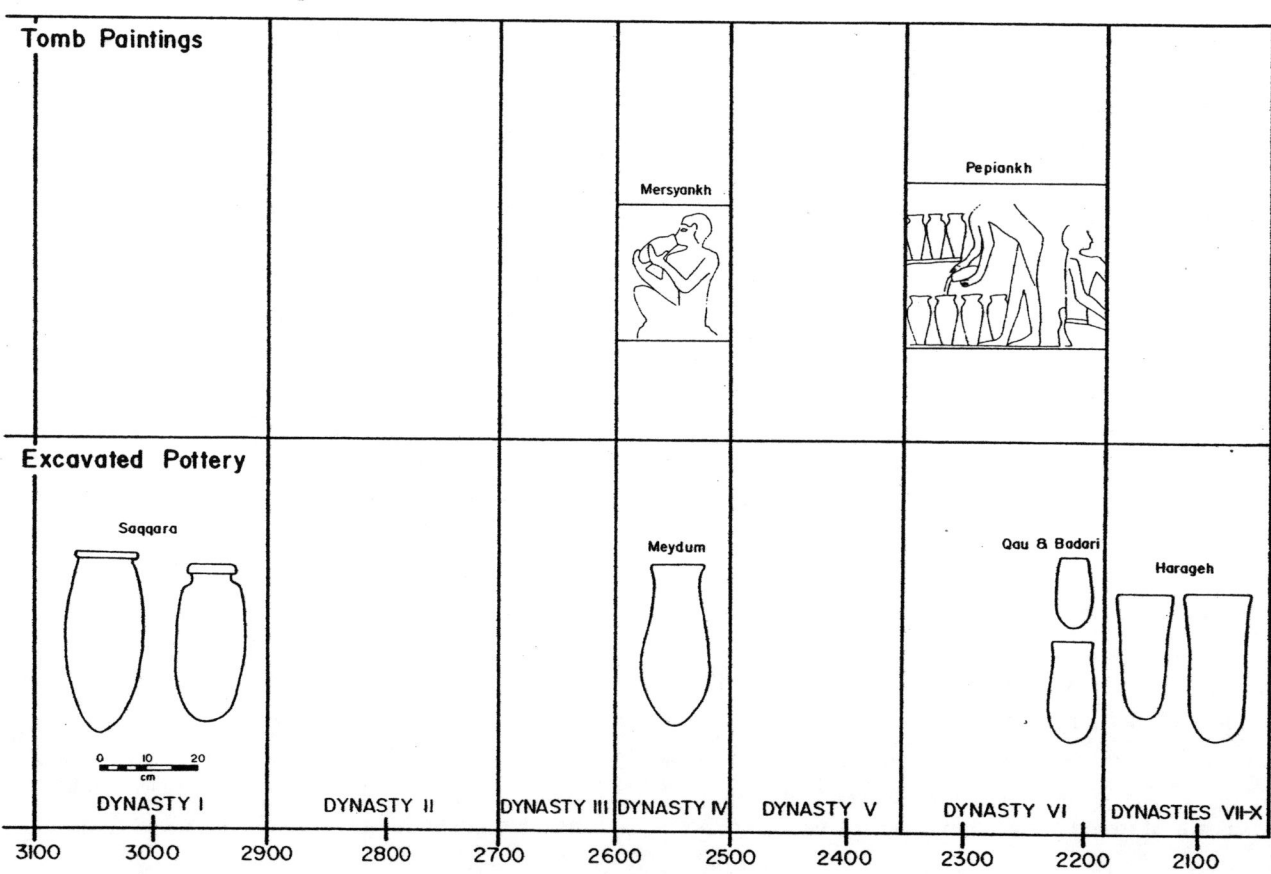

Pouring and Drinking Vessels (Figure 16a, 16b)

The essential feature of Egyptian pouring vessels as seen in the tomb paintings is the wide mouth. The situlae or beakers are cylindrical in shape with rounded bases. They have no neck, although some may have an outward flaring mouth. These vessels are found at all periods, with the exception of Dynasties I-III. At this early stage, a similar function may have been performed by jars with a short neck and slightly everted rolled rim. They have the same general shape, and the mouth is wide enough to facilitate pouring. At each stage thereafter, the excavated pouring jars range from outward flaring rim in Dynasties IV-XIII to those with a slightly inward leaning stance from the XVIIIth and XIXth Dynasties. These vessels have a size range from 20-30 cm. (Larger jars of similar shape existed but they would not have been used for drinking - their large size would have made them unmanagable for that purpose.) These wide mouthed jars have all been depicted in the tomb paintings fulfilling the dual functions of pouring and drinking.

Conclusions

Scenes of daily life depicted on the walls of ancient Egyptian tombs are most useful as an ethnographic source for the function of certain pottery forms and in helping to identify activity areas found in excavation. The pottery illustrated in tombs can be used as a broad chronological indicator. However, in many cases, the forms can not be separated further than Old, Middle, or New Kingdom. Some vessels may be assigned to a particular Dynasty, but only rarely can they be refined any further. This could partly be due to conservative pottery traditions in Egypt, and partly to sketchy representations in the tomb paintings.

FIGURE 16b   Pouring Vessels

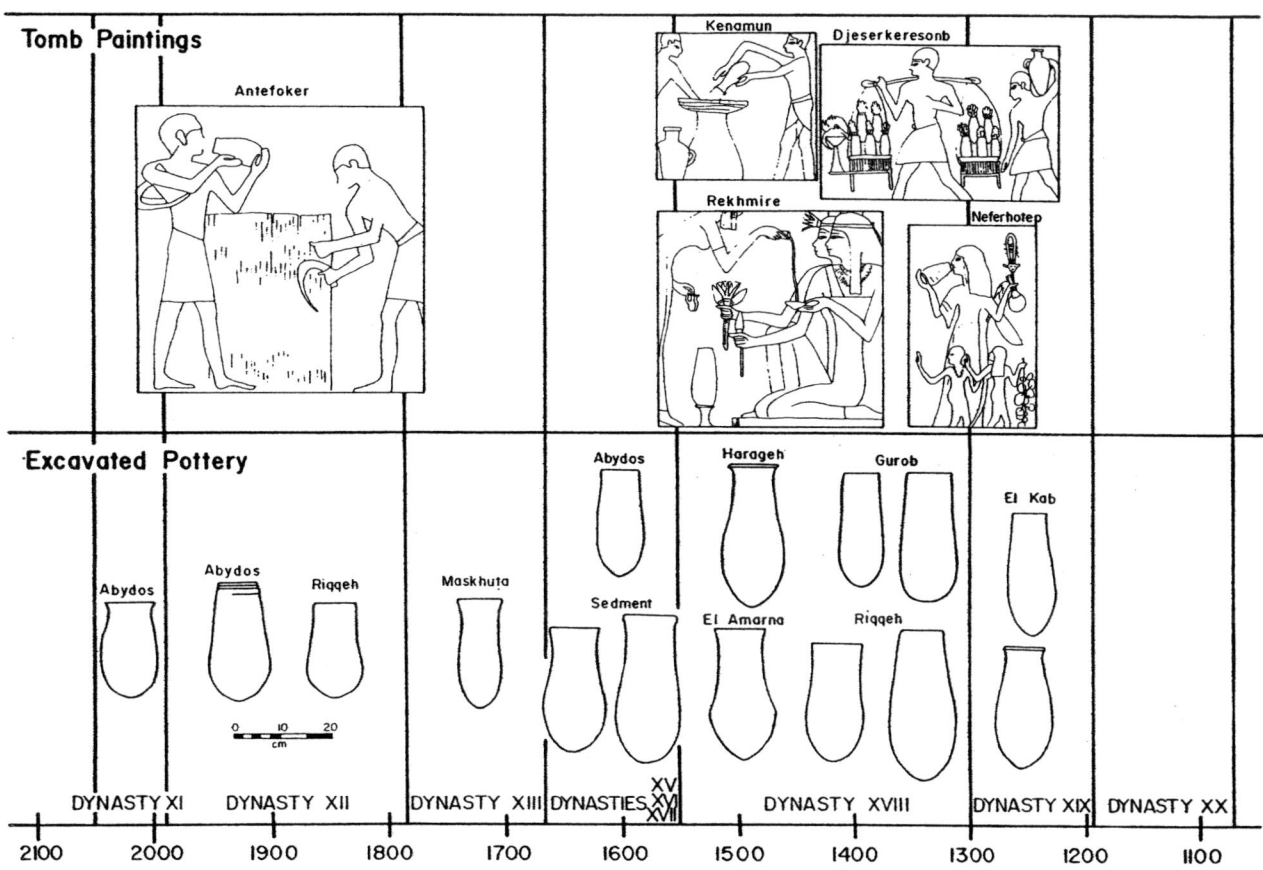

However, the conservatism of domestic pottery apparent in the tomb scenes is reinforced when examples of excavated pottery are included in the investigation. Chronological changes in a particular functional type are reflected in the representations of that type of vessel in the tomb paintings. These changes are gradual so that the continual use of general functional shapes can be traced over very long periods of time. From a theoretical perspective it may be suggestive that once a general shape of vessel has been found to work for a particular function there is little incentive to change it. The pace of change is slow indeed.

Fernand Braudel has explained how the underlying structures of the *longue durée* can get in the way of history and hinder its flow.

Just think of the difficulties of breaking out of certain geographical frameworks, certain biological realities, certain limits of productivity, even particular spiritual constraints: mental frameworks too can form prisons of the *longue durée*.[41]

This sentence could have been written specially for Egypt - a society isolated by reasons of geography; a society firmly anchored to its "black land", the land irrigated by the Nile river; a society with the most dependable seasonal cycle of agriculture made possible by the regular flooding of the Nile; a society with a rigid framework of bureaucracy; a society with an all-pervading religious structure; a society with a strong sense of its own identity. The persistence of certain pottery forms is but one outward sign of the stability inherent in a such a society. Noticeable changes in pottery forms tended to come as a result of outside influence during periods of extensive trade with Egypt's neighbours. For example borrowed forms from Canaan are most in evidence during the Old Kingdom with the use of ledge-handled store jars and spouted jugs with handles, and during the XVIIIth Dynasty with the popularity of the two-handled Canaanite store jar.

The usual aim of a pottery study is to demonstrate clearly why one assemblage of pottery is different from another and to stress the differences in form which can give chronological clues to the archaeologist. This investigation has turned the usual procedure upside-down by stressing features which do not change. It is these features that point both to the vessel's function and to the conservative traditions associated with daily subsistence and rhythmic, seasonal activities.

NOTES

1. This article benefits enormously from the contributions of Julia E. Pfaff who drew Figures 4-6, 8, 10, 12-16 and Loretta M. James who drew Figures 7 and 9.

2. Fernand Braudel, *On History*. Chicago: University of Chicago Press, 1980: 27.

3. Braudel, 1980: 3.

4. Many tombs have no scenes of daily life in their wall decoration. In some cases this absence may have been due to incomplete preservation, but in others it was clear that the decorative themes were purely religious or formal in character.

5. An early version of this paper was prepared for a Symposium on "Ancient Mediterranean Food Systems" during the Annual Meeting of the American Schools of Oriental Research, Anaheim: 1985.

6. Dynasty V: Akhethetep, PL.XVII; Dynasty VI: Asa, PL.XIX; Dynasty XI: Kemsit; Dynasty XII: Senbi, PL.XI; Dynasty XVIII: Ramose, PL.XXV.

7. Dynasty V: Nianchchnum and Chnumhotep, Abb.8; Dynasty XII: Khnumhotep, PL.XXIX; Tehutihetep, PL.XXVI; Dynasty XVIII: Ramose, PL.XXV.

8. Dynasty IV: Mersyankh, Fig.11; Dynasty V: Ti, PL.86; Dynasty VI: Asa, PL.XX; Dynasty XI: Baqt III, PL.VI; Dynasty XII: Antefoker, PL.XII; Dynasty XVIII: Rekhmire, PL.XLIX, L; Kenamun, PL.LVIII.

9. It would seem that these tasks usually were performed in adjacent areas.

10. Pepiankh the Middle, PL.XIII.

11. Pepiankh the middle, PL.XIII.

12. Antefoker, PL.XI.

13. Dynasty IV: Mersyankh, Fig.11; Dynasty V: Akhethetep, PL.XI; Dynasty VI: Khenty, Fig.42, PL.11; Khentika, PL.IX; Dynasty XII: Antefoker, PL.XI; Dynasty XVIII: Nebamun (No. 17), PL.XXII

14. As a matter of some historical interest, it may be noted that there are certain resemblances between the Egyptian pottery illustrated in tombs of the Vth and VIth Dynasties and that of excavated pottery of contemporary Early Bronze IV in Palestine. Given that similar specialized shapes probably were adapted to similar functions, it seems reasonable to suggest that the spouted vessels called "teapots" in Syro-Palestinian studies should really be called "beer pots".

15. Kenamun, PL.LVIII.

16. Dhout, PL.IV.

17. Amenmose (No. 42), PL.XXXVIII.

18. Amenemhet, PL.XXVI.

19. Dynasty IV: Mersyankh, Fig.11; Dynasty V: Nianchchnum and Chnumhotep, Abb. 16; Dynasty XI: Khety, PL.XVI; Dynasty XII: Amenemhat, PL.XII; Dynasty XVIII: Rekhmire, PL.XLV; Nakht, PL.XXII, XXIII; Parennefer, PL.XXVIII.C.; Dynasty XIX: Apy, PL.XXX, XXXIII.

20. e.g. Nefer and Ka-Hay, PL.9; Pepiankh, PL.XX.

21. A probable scenario for the interareal trade between Egypt and Palestine in the Early Bronze Age is described by Ruth Amiran in *Early Arad*, 1978: 114-115.

22. Rekhmire, PL.XLIX, L.

23. Virginia Grace, "The Canaanite Jar" in *The Aegean and the Near East, Studies presented to Hetty Goldman*. ed. Saul S. Weinberg, New York: 1956. pp.80-109; PL.IX-XII.

24. N. de Garis Davies and R. O. Faulkner, "A Syrian Trading Venture to Egypt". *Journal of Egyptian Archaeology* 33 (1947) PL.VIII.

25. Kenamun, PL.XIX

26. Rekhmire, PL.XXXIV.

27. Rekhmire, PL.XLVIII, XL; Amenmose PL.XXII.

28. Rekhmire, PL. LVIII.

29. Nakht, PL.XXII, XXIII, XXVI; Paheri, PL.IV; Rekhmire, PL.XLVI.

30. Dynasty V: Urarna, PL.X; Dynasty VI: Shedu, PL.XXV; Dynasty XII: Antefoker, PL.VIII.

31. Dynasty IV: Mersyankh, Fig.11; Dynasty XII: Antefoker, PL.III; Dynasty XVIII: Rekhmire, PL.42; Djeserkeresonb, PL.1; Neferhotep, PL.XIV.

32. For the suggestion that these juglets contained a lotus concentrate with narcotic properties, see W. Benson Harer, "Pharmacological and Biological Properties of the Egyptian Lotus". *J.A.R.C.E.* XXII (1985) pp.49-54.

33. Antefoker, PL.XII; Amenemhat, PL.XII.

34. Antefoker, PL.XI; Khnumhotep, PL.XXIX.

35. Amenemhat, PL.XI.

36. Khnumhotep, PL.XXX.

37. Unpublished excavation data from the Wadi Tumilat Project directed by J.S.Holladay. See also the bread moulds and baking trays found in association with XVIIIth Dynasty baking areas at Tell el–Amarna: Barry Kemp, *Journal of Egyptian Archaeology* 65:5-12.

38. Personal communication from M.A.W. Van Dusen, Ph.D. candidate, University of Toronto.

39. The pictorial representations from the tombs show only the external appearance of the vessel at a distance. In the case of the drawings from early excavations, this is not necessarily a handicap for comparison, since most of these drawings were rendered without benefit of sections and therefore can be compared directly to the tomb depictions.

40. For a typology of excavated bread moulds see Helen Jacqet–Gordon, "A Tentative Typology of Egyptian Bread Moulds" in *Studien zur altägyptischen Keramik*, ed. Dorothea Arnold. Mainz am Rhein: 1981.

41. Braudel, p.31.

APPENDIX A: CATALOGUE OF SCENES IN EGYPTIAN TOMBS WHICH DEPICT POTTERY IN USE

OLD KINGDOM TOMBS

ABA   (Deir el Gebrawi No.8) .... Nomarch
VIth Dynasty: Pepy II.
Davies, N. de G., *The Rock Tombs of Deir el Gebrawi*. Vol.I. 1902.

AKHETHETEP   .... Vizier
Vth Dynasty: Djed-ka-re.
Davies, N. de G., *The Mastaba of Ptahhetep and Akhethetep II*, 1901.

ASA   (Deir el Gebrawi No.72) .... Nomarch
VIth Dynasty.
Davies, N. de G., *The Rock Tombs of Deir el Gebrawi*. Vol.II. 1902.

IDU   (Giza 7102) .... Overseer of the Meret-serfs
VIth Dynasty: Pepy II.
Simpson, W. K., *The Mastabas of Qar and Idu*. 1976.

KHENTIKA   .... Vizier
VIth Dynasty: Teti - Pepy I
James, T. G. H., *The Mastaba of Khentika called Ikeki*. 1953.

KHENTY   (Thebes No.405) .... Chancellor of the King
VIth Dynasty.
Saleh, Mohammed, *Three Old Kingdom Tombs at Thebes*. 1977.

MERA   .... Priestess of Hathor
VIth Dynasty.
Petrie, W. M. F., *Deshasheh*. 1898.

MERSYANKH III   (Giza 7530) .... Grand daughter of Cheops. Daughter of Hetepheres
IVth Dynasty: Chephren, Mycerinus.
Dunham, D. and Simpson, W. K., *The Mastaba of Queen Mersyankh III*. 1974.

NEFER AND KA-HAY .... Inspector of the Singers
Vth Dynasty: Ne-user-re.
Moussa, A. M. and Altenmuller, H., *The Tomb of Nefer and Ka-Hay*. 1971.

NIANCHCHNUM AND CHNUMHOTEP .... Priest of Re
Vth Dynasty: Ne-user-re.
Moussa, A. M., *Das Grab des Nianchnum und Chnumhotep*. 1977.

PEPI   (D. No.1)
                VIth Dynasty
                Blackman, A. M. and Apted, M. R., *The Rock Tombs of Meir, V.* 1953.

PEPIANKH   (A. No.2) . . . . Governor, Treasurer of the King of Lower Egypt
                VIth Dynasty: Pepy II.
                Blackman. A. M. and Apted, M. R., *The Rock Tombs of Meir V.* 1953.

PEPIANKH the middle (D. No.2) . . . . Vizier, Superintendent of Upper Egypt
                VIth Dynasty: Pepy II.
                Blackman, A. M., *The Rock Tombs of Meir IV.* 1924.

PTAHHETEP   Vth Dynasty: Djed-ka-re.
                Davies, N. de G., *The Mastaba of Ptahhetep and Akhethetep.* Vol.I. 1900.

SHEDU   VIth Dynasty: Teti.
                Petrie, W. M. F., *Deshasheh.* 1898.

TI   Vth Dynasty.
                Steindorff, *Das Grab des Ti.* 1913.

URARNA   (Sheik Said No.25) . . . . Royal Acquaintance. Governor of the Great House
                Vth Dynasty: Ne-user-re.
                Davies, N. de G., *The Rock Tombs of Sheik Said.* 1901.

ZAU   . . . . Great Chief of the Nome of This
                VIth Dynasty: Pepy II.
                Davies, N. de G., *The Rock Tombs of Deir el Gebrawi.* Vol. II. 1902.

MIDDLE KINGDOM TOMBS

AMENEMHAT   (Beni Hasan No.2) . . . . Great Chief of the Oryx Nome
                XIIth Dynasty: Senwosret I.
                Newberry, Percy E., *Beni Hasan I.* 1893.

ANTEFOKER   (Thebes No.60) . . . . Vizier
                XIIth Dynasty: Senwosret I.
                Davies, N. de G., *The Tomb of Antefoker.* 1920.

BAQT II   (Beni Hasan No.33) . . . . Great Chief of the Oryx Nome
                XIth Dynasty.
                Newberry, Percy E., *Beni Hasan II.* 1893.

BAQT III   (Beni Hasan No.15) . . . . Governor of the Oryx Nome
                  XIth Dynasty.
                  Newberry, Percy E., *Beni Hasan II*. 1893.

DAGA   (Thebes No.103) . . . . Vizier
                  XI - XIIth Dynasties.
                  Davies, N. de G., *Five Theban Tombs*. 1913.

KEMSIT   (Deir el-Bahari) . . . . Princess
                  XIth Dynasty.
                  Naville, E., *Deir el-Bahari III*. 1913.

KHETY   (Beni Hasan No.17) . . . . Governor of the Oryx Nome. Son of Baqt III
                  XIth Dynasty.
                  Newberry, Percy E., *Beni Hasan II*. 1893.

KHNUMHOTEP   (Beni Hasan No.3) . . . . Administrator of the Eastern Desert
                  XIIth Dynasty: Senwosret II.
                  Newberry, Percy E., *Beni Hasan I*. 1893.

SENBI   (B. No.4) . . . . Nomarch
                  XIIth Dynasty: Amenemhet I.
                  Blackman, A. M., *The Rock Tombs of Meir I*. 1914.

TEHUTIHOTEP   (El Bersheh No.2) . . . . Sole Royal Friend
                  XIIth Dynasty: Senwosret II, Senwosret III.
                  Newberry, Percy E., *El Bersheh I*. 1892.

NEW KINGDOM TOMBS

AHMES   . . . . Steward of the House of Akhenaten
                  XVIIIth Dynasty: Akhenaten.
                  Davies, N. de G., *The Rock Tombs of El Amarna III*. 1905.

AMENEMHET   (Thebes No.82) . . . . Scribe, Steward of the Vizier
                  XVIIIth Dynasty: Tuthmosis III.
                  Davies, Nina de G., *The Tomb of Amenemhet*. 1915.

AMENHOTPE-SI-SE   (Thebes No.75) . . . . Second Priest of Amun
                  XVIIIth Dynasty: Tuthmosis IV.
                  Davies, N. de G., *The Tombs of Two Officials of Tuthmosis IV*. 1923.

AMENMOSE   (Thebes No.42) . . . . Captain of Infantry
                  XVIIIth Dynasty: Tuthmosis III.
                  Davies, N. de Garis, *The Tombs of Menkheperrasonb, Amenmose, and another*. 1933.

AMENMOSE   (Thebes No.89) . . . . Steward
                  XVIIIth Dynasty: Tuthmosis III, Amenophis III.
                  Davies, N.M. and N. de G., "The Tomb of Amenmose at Thebes." *J.E.A.* 26:131f.
                  (1940)

ANTEF   (Thebes No.155) . . . . Great Herald
                  XVIIIth Dynasty: Hatshepsut, Tuthmosis III.
                  Save-Soderbergh, Torgny, *Four Eighteenth Dynasty Tombs.* 1957.

APY   (Thebes No.217) . . . . Sculptor of Amun
                  XIXth Dynasty: Ramesses II.
                  Davies, N. de G., *Two Ramesside Tombs at Thebes.* 1927.

AY   . . . . Father of the Divinity
                  XVIIIth Dynasty: Akhenaten.
                  Davies, N. de G., *The Rock Tombs of El Amarna. VI.* 1908.

BENJA   (Thebes No.343) . . . . Overseer of Works
                  XVIIIth Dynasty: Hatshepsut, Tuthmosis III, Amenophis II.
                  Guksch, Heike, *Das Grab des Benja, gen. Paheqamen.* 1978.

DHOUT   (Thebes No.45) . . . . Head of the Weavers of the Temple of Amun
                  XVIIIth Dynasty: Tuthmosid.
                  Davies, N. de G., *Seven Private Tombs at Kurnah.* 1948.

DJESERKERESONB   (Thebes No.38) . . . . Steward of the Granary of Amun
                  XVIIIth Dynasty: Tuthmosis IV.
                  Davies, N.M. de G., *Scenes from some Theban Tombs.* 1963.

HUYA   . . . . Steward of the House of Queen Tyi
                  XVIIIth Dynasty: Akhenaten.
                  Davies, N. de G., *The Rock Tombs of El Amarna. III.* 1905.

KENAMUN   (Thebes No.162) . . . . Chief Steward, Mayor of Thebes
                  XVIIIth Dynasty: Amenophis II.
                  Davies, N. de G., *The Tomb of Kenamun at Thebes.* 1930.

KHONS   (Thebes No.31) . . . . Mortuary Priest of Tuthmosis III
                  XVIIIth Dynasty: Tutankhamun (?)
                  Davies, N. de G., *Seven Private Tombs at Kurnah.* 1948.

MAHU   . . . . Chief of Police
                  XVIIIth Dynasty: Akhenaten.
                  Davies, N. de G., *The Rock Tombs at El Amarna. IV.* 1906.

MENKHEPERRESONB (Thebes No.86) .... High Priest of Amun
                      XVIIIth Dynasty: Tuthmosis III, Amenophis II.
                      Davies, N. de G., *The Tombs of Menkheperresonb, Amenmose, and another*. 1933.

MENTUHERKHEPSHEF (Thebes No.20) .... Mayor of Aphritopolis
                      XVIIIth Dynasty: Tuthmosis III (?)
                      Davies, N. de G., *Five Theban Tombs*. 1913.

MERYRA   XVIIIth Dynasty: Akhenaten.
                      Davies, N. de G., *The Rock Tombs of El Amarna. I*. 1903.

NAKHT   (Thebes No.52) .... Serving Priest of Amun
                      XVIIIth Dynasty: Amenophis II, Tuthmosis IV.
                      Davies, N. de G., *The Tomb of Nakht at Thebes*. 1917.

NAKHTAMUN   (Thebes No.341) .... Overseer of the Altar
                      XIXth Dynasty: Ramesses II.
                      Davies, N. de G., *Seven Private Tombs at Kurnah*. 1948.

NEBAMUN   (Thebes No.17) .... Chief Physician
                      XVIIIth Dynasty: Amenophis II (?)
                      Save-Soderbergh, Torgny, *Four Eighteenth Dynasty Tombs*. 1957.

NEBAMUN   (Thebes No.90) .... Captain of Police
                      XVIIIth Dynasty: Tuthmosis IV.
                      Davies, N. de G., *The Tombs of Two Officials of Tuthmosis the Fourth*. 1923.

NEFERHOTEP   (Thebes No.49) .... Superintendent of the Oxen and Heifers of Amun
                      XVIIIth Dynasty: Ay.
                      Davies, N. de G., *The Tomb of Neferhotep at Thebes*. 1933.

PAHERI   .... Nomarch
                      XVIIIth Dynasty: Tuthmosis II, Hatshepsut, Tuthmosis III.
                      Tylor, J. J. and Griffith, F. LL., *The Tomb of Paheri at El Kab*. 1894.

PARENNEFER   .... Craftsman of the King
                      XVIIIth Dynasty: Akhenaten.
                      Davies, N. de G., *The Rock Tombs of El Amarna VI*. 1908.

RAMOSE   .... Vizier
                      XVIIIth Dynasty: Akhenaten.
                      Davies, N. de G., *The Tomb of the Vizier Ramose*. 1941.

REKHMIRE   (Thebes No.100) .... Vizier
                      XVIIIth Dynasty: Tuthmosis III, Amenophis II.
                      Davies, N. de G., *The Tomb of Rekhmire at Thebes*. 1943.

TJANUNI (Thebes No.74) . . . . Seal-bearer
XVIIIth Dynasty: Tuthmosis III, Amenophis II, Tuthmosis IV.
Brack, Annelies und Artur, *Das Grab des Tjanuni*. 1977.

TUTU . . . . Chamberlain, Overseer of Works, Overseer of the Treasury
XVIIIth Dynasty: Akhenaten.
Davies, N. de G., *The Rock Tombs of El Amarna VI*. 1908.

BIBLIOGRAPHY

TOMB ILLUSTRATIONS

BALCZ, H.   1933   "Die Gefussdardtellungen des Alten Reiches". *MDAIK* IV:207f.

BLACKMAN, A. M.   1914   *The Rock Tombs of Meir I*. Archaeological Survey of Egypt, Memoir 22. London: Egypt Exploration Fund.

BLACKMAN, A. M.   1924   *The Rock Tombs of Meir IV*. Archaeological Survey of Egypt, Memoir 25. London: Egypt Exploration Fund.

BLACKMAN, A. M.   1953   *The Rock Tombs of Meir V*. Archaeological Survey of Egypt, Memoir 28. London: Egypt Exploration Society.

BRACK, A. & A.   1977   *Das Grab des Tjanuni. Theben Nr.74. Archaologische Veröffentlichungen*. 19. Mainz am Rhein: Verlag Philipp von Zabern.

DAVIES, N. de G.   1900   *The Mastaba of Ptahhetep and Akhethetep I*. Archaeological Survey of Egypt, Memoir 8. London: Egypt Exploration Fund.

DAVIES, N. de G.   1901   *The Mastaba of Ptahhetep and Akhethetep II*. Archaeological Survey of Egypt, Memoir 9. London: Egypt Exploration Fund.

DAVIES, N. de G.   1901   *The Rock Tombs of Sheik Said*. Archaeological Survey of Egypt, Memoir 10. London: Egypt Exploration Fund.

DAVIES, N. de G.   1902   *The Rock Tombs of Deir el Gebrawi I*. Archaeological Survey of Egypt, Memoir 11. London: Egypt Exploration Fund.

DAVIES, N. de G.   1902   *The Rock Tombs of Deir el Gebrawi II*. Archaeological Survey of Egypt, Memoir 12. London: Egypt Exploration Fund.

DAVIES, N. de G.   1903   *The Rock Tombs of El Amarna I*. Archaeological Survey of Egypt, Memoir 13. London: Egypt Exploration Fund.

DAVIES, N. de G.   1905   *The Rock Tombs of El Amarna III*. Archaeological Survey of Egypt, Memoir 15. London: Egypt Exploration Fund.

DAVIES, N. de G.   1906   *The Rock Tombs of El Amarna IV*. Archaeological Survey of Egypt, Memoir 16. London: Egypt Exploration Fund.

DAVIES, N. de G.   1908   *The Rock Tombs of El Amarna VI*. Archaeological Survey of Egypt, Memoir 18. London: Egypt Exploration Fund.

DAVIES, N. de G.   1913   *Five Theban Tombs*. Archaeological Survey of Egypt, Memoir 21.
                                  London: Egypt Exploration Fund.

DAVIES, N. de G.   1915   *The Tomb of Amenemhet*. The Theban Tombs Series, First Memoir.
                                  London: Egypt Exploration Fund.

DAVIES, N. de G.   1917   *The Tomb of Nakht at Thebes. No.52*. New York: Metropolitan
                                  Museum of Art.

DAVIES, N. de G.   1920   *The Tomb of Antefoker and his wife Senet*. The Theban Tombs
                                  Series, Second Memoir. London: George Allen and Unwin, Ltd.

DAVIES, N. de G.   1923   *The Tombs of Two Officials of Tuthmosis the Fourth*. The Theban
                                  Tombs Series, Third Memoir. London: George Allen and Unwin,
                                  Ltd.

DAVIES, N. de G.   1927   *Two Ramesside Tombs at Thebes*. New York: Metropolitan
                                  Museum of Art.

DAVIES, N. de G.   1928   "Akhenaten at Thebes" *Journal of Egyptian Archaeology* IX:132f.

DAVIES, N. de G.   1930   *The Tomb of Kenamun at Thebes. Vol I*. Egyptian Expedition.
                                  Publication 5.
                                  New York: Metropolitan Museum of Art

DAVIES, N. de G.   1933   *The Tombs of Menkheperrasonb, Amenmose, and another*. The
                                  Theban Tombs Series, Fifth Memoir. London: Egypt Exploration
                                  Society.

DAVIES, N. de G.   1933   *The Tomb of Neferhotep at Thebes. Vol. I*. Publications. Vol. IX.
                                  New York: Metropolitan Museum of Art.

DAVIES, N. M. & N. de G. 1940   "The Tomb of Amenmose (No.89) at Thebes". *Journal of Egyptian
                                  Archaeology* 26:131f.

DAVIES, N. de G.   1941   *The Tomb of the Vizier Ramose*. Mond Excavations at Thebes 1.
                                  London: The Egypt Exploration Society.

DAVIES, N. de G.   1943   *The Tomb of Rekhmire at Thebes. Vol. I*. Publication. Vol. XI. New
                                  York: Metropolitan Museum of Art.

DAVIES, N. de G.   1948   *Seven Private Tombs at Kurnah*. Mond Excavations at Thebes 11.
                                  London: Egypt Exploration Society.

DAVIES, N.M. de G.   1963   *Scenes from some Theban Tombs*. Private Tombs at Thebes. Vol.
                                  IV. Oxford: The Griffith Institute.

DUNHAM, D. & SIMPSON, W. K.
>1974   *The Mastaba of Queen Mersyankh III.*
>Boston: Museum of Fine Arts.

GUSCH, H.   1978   *Das Grab des Benja, gen. Paheqamen. Theben Nr. 343.*
Archäologische Veröffentlichungen 7. Mainz am Rhein: Verlag
Philipp von Zabern.

JAMES, T. G. H.   1953   *The Mastaba of Khentika called Ikhekhi.* Archaeological Survey of
Egypt, Memoir 30. London: Egypt Exploration Society.

KLEBS, L.   1914   *Die Reliefs und Mälerein des Alten Reiches.* Heidelberg: Carl
Winters Universitats Buchhandlung.

KLEBS, L.   1922   *Die Reliefs und Mälerein des Mittleren Reiches.* Heidelberg:
CarlWinters Universitats Buchhandlung.

KLEBS, L.   1932   *Die Reliefs und Mälerein des Neuen Reiches.* Heidelberg: Carl
Winters Universitats Buchhandlung.

MOUSSA, A. M. & ALTENMÜLLER, H.
>1971   *The Tomb of Nefer and Ka-Hay.* *Archäologische Veröffentlichungen*
>5. Mainz am Rhein: Verlag Philipp von Zabern.

MOUSSA, A. M.   1977   *Das Grab des Nianchchnum und Chnumhotep.* *Archaologische
Veroffentlichungen* 21. Mainz am Rhein: Verlag Philipp von Zabern.

NAVILLE, E.   1913   *The XIth Dynasty Temple at Deir El-Bahari. Part III.* Thirty-Second
Memoir. London: Egypt Exploration Fund.

NEWBERRY, P. E.   1893   *Beni Hasan Part I.* Archaeological Survey of Egypt, Memoir 1.
London: Egypt Exploration Fund.

NEWBERRY, P. E.   1893   *Beni Hasan Part II.* Archaeological Survey of Egypt, Memoir 2.
London: Egypt Exploration Fund.

NEWBERRY, P. E.   1894   *El Bersheh. Part I.* Archaeological Survey of Egypt, Memoir 3.
London: Egypt Exploration Fund.

PETRIE, W. M. F.   1898   *Deshasheh.* Memoir 15. London: Egypt Exploration Fund.

SALEH, M.   1977   *Three Old Kingdom Tombs at Thebes. Archaologische
Veroffentlichungen* 14. Mainz am Rhein: Verlag Philipp von
Zabern.

SÄVE-SÖDERBERGH, T. 1957 *Four Eighteenth Dynasty Tombs*. Private Tombs at Thebes Vol. I. Oxford: The Griffith Institute.

SIMPSON, W. K. 1976 *The Mastabas of Qar and Idu*. Boston: Museum of Fine Arts.

STEINDORFF, G. 1913 *Das Grab des Ti*. Leipzig: J. C. Hinrichd'sche Buchhandlung.

TYLOR, J. J. & GRIFFITH, F. LL.
1894 *The Tomb of Paheri at El Kab*. Memoir 11. London: Egypt Exploration Fund.

POTTERY

BRUNTON, G. 1927 *Qau and Badari I*. London: British School of Archaeology in Egypt, 44.

BRUNTON, G. 1928 *Qau and Badari II*. London: British School of Archaeology in Egypt, 45.

BRUNTON, G. 1938 *Qau and Badari III*. London: British School of Archaeology in Egypt, 50.

ENGELBACH, R. 1915 *Riqqeh and Memphis VI*. London: British School of Archaeology in Egypt, 25.

ENGELBACH, R. 1923 *Harageh*. London: British School of Archaeology in Egypt, 28.

FRANKFORT, K. & PENDLEBURY, J. D. S.
1933 *The City of Akhenaten, Part II, The North Suburb and the Desert Altars*. Memoir 40. London: Egypt Exploration Society.

GARSTANG, J. 1902 *Mahasna and Bet Khallaf*. London: British School of Archaeology in Egypt, 7.

HOLLADAY, J. S. n.d. Tell el Maskhuta. Unpublished material.

KELLEY, A. 1976 *The Pottery of Ancient Egypt*. Toronto: The Royal Ontario Museum.

KEMP, B. J. 1978 "Preliminary Report on the El-Amarna Survey 1978" *Journal of Egyptian Archaeology* 65:5-12.

MOND, R. & MYERS, O. H.
1937 *Cemeteries of Armant I*. Memoir 42. London: Egypt Exploration Society.

NAVILLE, E. & GRIFFITH, F. LL.
1890 *The Mound of the Jew and the City of Onias; The Antiquities of Tell el-Yahudiyeh*. Memoir 7. London: Egypt Exploration Fund.

PEET, T. E. & WOOLLEY, C. L.
1923 *The City of Akhenaten, Part I*. Memoir 38. London: Egypt Exploration Society.

PENDLEBURY. J. D. S. 1951 *The City of Akhenaten, Part III*. Memoir 44. London: Egypt Exploration Society.

PETRIE, W. M. F. 1890 *Kahun, Gurob and Hawara*. London: Kegan Trench, Trubner and Company.

PETRIE, W. M. F. 1897 *Six Temples at Thebes*. London: Bernard Quaritch.

PETRIE, W. M. F. 1900a *Dendereh*. Memoir 17. London: Egypt Exploration Fund.

PETRIE, W. M. F. 1900b *The Royal Tombs of the First Dynasty, Part I*. Memoir 18. London: Egypt Exploration Fund.

PETRIE, W. M. F. 1902 *Abydos I*. Memoir 22. London: Egypt Exploration Fund.

PETRIE, W. M. F. 1903 *Abydos II*. Memoir 24. London: Egypt Exploration Fund.

PETRIE, W. M. F. 1909 *Qurneh*. London: British School of Archaeology in Egypt, 16.

PETRIE, W. M. F., MACKAY, E., & WAINWRIGHT, W.
1910 *Meydum and Memphis III*. London: British School of Archaeology in Egypt, 18.

PETRIE, W. M. F. & MACKAY, E.
1915 *Heliopolis, Kafr Ammar, and Shurafa*. London: British School of Archaeology in Egypt, 24.

PETRIE, W. M. F. & BRUNTON, G.
1924a *Sedment I*. London: British School of Archaeology in Egypt, 34.

PETRIE, W. M. F. & BRUNTON, G.
1924b *Sedment II*. London: British School of Archaeology in Egypt, 35.

QUIBELL, J. E. 1898 *El Kab*. London: British School of Archaeology in Egypt, 3.

QUIBELL, J. E. 1900 *Hierakonpolis I*. London: British School of Archaeology in Egypt, 4.

REISNER, G. A. 1955 *A History of the Giza Necropolis, II. The Tomb of Hetep-heres, the Mother of Cheops*. Cambridge: University Press.